EARLY RECORDS OF FISHING CREEK PRESBYTERIAN CHURCH

Chester County, South Carolina 1799-1859

With Appendices of the Visitation List of
Rev. John Simpson, 1774-1776
and the Cemetery Roster, 1762-1979

Compiled by
Brent H. Holcomb and Elmer O. Parker

HERITAGE BOOKS
2008

HERITAGE BOOKS
AN IMPRINT OF HERITAGE BOOKS, INC.

Books, CDs, and more—Worldwide

For our listing of thousands of titles see our website
at
www.HeritageBooks.com

A Facsimile Reprint
Published 2008 by
HERITAGE BOOKS, INC.
Publishing Division
100 Railroad Ave. #104
Westminster, Maryland 21157

— Publisher's Notice —
In reprints such as this, it is often not possible to remove blemishes from the original. We feel the contents of this book warrant its reissue despite these blemishes and hope you will agree and read it with pleasure.

International Standard Book Numbers
Paperbound: 978-1-55613-507-1
Clothbound: 978-0-7884-7192-6

INTRODUCTION

This volume is comprised of three sections: records of the session 1799 - 1859, the visitation list of Rev. John Simpson 1774 - 1776, and the cemetery 1762 - 1979. The first two sections are facsimiles of the originals. Our thanks goes to the session of Fishing Creek Presbyterian Church for their permission to include the minutes and to South Carolina Library for their permission to publish the visitation list.

The session records are obviously important for the baptisms, marriages, deaths and removals recorded therein. The visitation list is most important for placing these early members in family groups. The inclusion of the cemetery inscriptions needs no explanation. Mr. Elmer O. Parker and the writer have spent many hours in this churchyard to make an accurate reading of these names and dates.

Fishing Creek Presbyterian Church was organized about 1770. Its first bench of elders consisted of Samuel Neely, John Latta, Robert Walker and Robert Lusk. The Rev. John Simpson (1740 - 15 February 1808) of New Jersey was ordained and installed as pastor on 6 April 1774. He served the church until 1790 when he removed to Pendleton District, South Carolina. During the War for independence he was an active supporter of the patriot cause. On Saturday, June 10, 1780, Col. George Turnbull, the British commander at Rocky Mount, S.C. sent Capt. Christian Huck and a party of horsemen on a scout up Fishing Creek. When they kindled the fire that destroyed the home of the Rev. John Simpson, and Huck's co-horts Burrel and Jeremiah Burge carried off the bed clothes and other household articles, they ignited a torch of freedom that burned in the breasts of the minister and his congregation. His church at Fishing Creek became the rallying point of patriot resistance. Here gathered the McClures, Gastons, Gills, Walkers, Coopers, Kelseys, Porters, and their like, and formed themselves into companies under Captains John McClure, Alexander Campbell, Alexander Pagan, Lieutenants John Mills and Robert Cooper and joined General Thomas Sumter's partisan army.

It was a rule with Rev. Simpson to visit every family and member of his church during his pastorate. He instructed the adults and catechised the children. The visitation list is a record of these visits.

This volume is offered in hope that it will aid genealogists and historians interested in this area of South Carolina. This church is the first record of many early families of York and Chester counties, South Carolina.

Brent H. Holcomb, C. A. L. S.
Columbia, South Carolina

TABLE OF CONTENTS

Edwin R. Mills, a clerk of Fishing Creek Church.

Fishing Creek Presbyterian Church

A general view of the churchyard showing some of the older graves in the silent city of the dead.

Elizabeth Hartness, wife of John Smith Hartness was a daughter of John Cooper and Elizabeth Walker, daughter of Robert and Jane Walker.

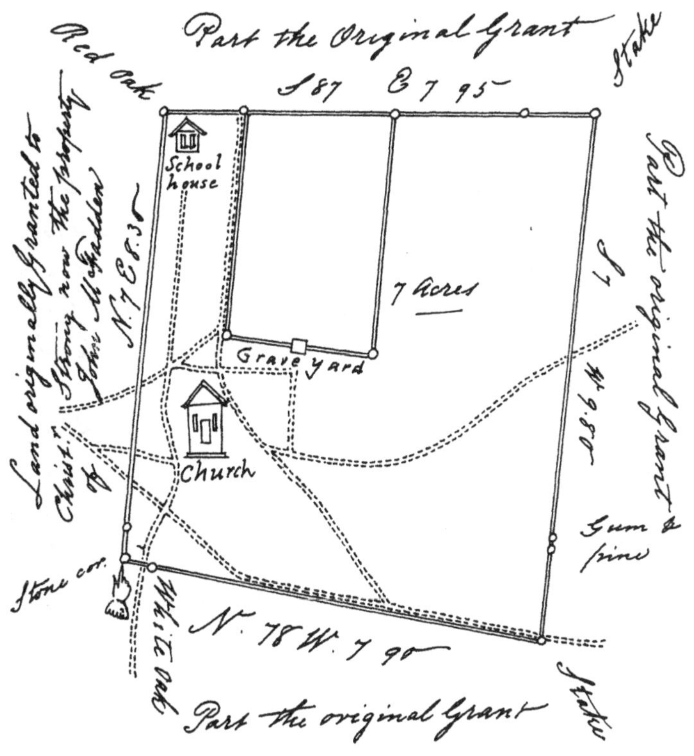

FISHING CREEK PRESBYTERIAN CHURCH AND GROUNDS

This tract of seven acres was deeded to the Rev. John B. Davies, pastor, and Major John Neely, elder, of the Fishing Creek Presbyterian Church Society, by John McFadden, October 6, 1826. It was part of 56 acres granted to George Kelsey, by George III., May 7, 1774.

Redrawn by Elmer Oris Parker from a plat by Thomas Reid, Deputy Surveyor.

Approved to 1838

"Unworthy Communicants are said 'to eat and drink Judgment to themselves', which I conceive, imports, 1. That the hurt which comes by unworthy communicating comes upon the person himself, not on Christ whose body and blood he is guilty of; for themselves has a relation not (primarily) to others, but to Christ.
They may eat Judgment to Ministers and Fellow Communicants, if they have a sinful hand in bringing them to the table."

Thomas Boston.

What a solemn thought for Church-sessions!

1

The Records of the Session of Fishing creek Church;

with

A brief Statement of its origin and progress compiled by its present Pastor, John B. Davies, acting as the clerk for the said Session

A brief Historical sketch of the Church of Fishing-creek, in Chester District S.C.

This church was organized about the year 1770. Of its first bench of Elders were Samuel Neely, John Latta, Robert Walker & Robert Lusk. In the year 1773 this church procured the labors of the Rev. John Simpson from New Jersey. He arrived at Fishing-creek on the 26th of November of that year. He was ordained and installed April 6th 1774 in the pastoral charge by the Presbytery of Orange, which embraced the States of North Carolina, South Carolina and Georgia. Mr Simpson sustained the relation of Pastor to this church in connexion with Lower Fishing-creek, afterwards, Richardson; But having withdrawn from that church, he continued the Pastor of this church until 1789, when this relation was dissolved. He however served the church for one year more and then removed to Pendelton District S.C. where he continued his ministerial labors until his death on February 4th 1808.

The congregation remained vacant, with the exception of a few months in 1793, (when they were supplied by Mr John Bowman, a licentiate of Orange Presbytery) until 1795. In September 1795 the Church prefered their call to Mr William G. Rosborough a Licentiate of the Presbytery of South Carolina, (which was organized in 1785). He took their call under consideration and labored amongst them for two years under considerable infirmity of body and at length was compelled to return their call.

In April 1798 this church gave an invitation to Mr John B. Davies to labor amongst them, as a supply. He was a Licentiate of the Presbytery of South Carolina. His labors proving acceptable, this church in union with Richardson presented their calls to Mr Davies to become their pastor. Mr Davies having accepted their calls he was ordained and installed as the Pastor of the two Churches May 14th 1799. His labors were devoted to the two churches for the space of thirty three years, when (1831) the pastoral charge of Richardson was resigned; but that of Fishing-creek retained and still continues (1839). When Mr Davies became Pastor of this church its bench of Elders were Samuel Neely, David Carr David Neely, Thomas Neely, Thomas Latta to whom were added in 1801 Mr Hugh Gaston.

In 1804 Thomas Neely, Thomas Latta, Hugh Gaston, Josiah Porter Charles Boggs, J. Wm ~~Walker D. Davis [illegible]~~ In 1808 Thomas Neely H. Gaston, Josiah Porter, Jas. Steele, Chs. Boyd, Jas. Wallis & Samuel Lewis. In 1812 T. Neely, H. Gaston, J. Porter Ch. Boyd, J. Wallis, S. Lewis, Jas. E. McFadden & John Boyd – In 1820. H. Gaston, C. Boyd. S. Lewis J. E. McFadden, J. Boyd William Bradford, Edward Crawford, Dr. A. Rosborough & John Neely

In 1827. C. Boyd. S. Lewis, J. Boyd, J. Neely, E. Crawford. Wm Stringfellow, Robert Miller, Alexr Gaston & Josiah H. Gill.

In 1835 C. Boyd, superannuated, E. Crawford, W. Stringfellow R. Miller, J. E. McFadden, Alexr Crawford & Wm Cowan.

In 1839. C. Boyd, Sup. E. Crawford, Robert Miller, J. E. McFadden A. Crawford, W. Cowan, John Poage & Geo. H. Neely. Revd. C. Gilland became pastor 1842—

In 1846. Robert Miller, Alex Crawford. John Poag. Geo. H. Neely John S. Chambers J. Henry Crawford. Robt Stringfellow.— Revd. R. Miller became Pastor 1849—

In 1851. Robert Miller, John Poag, Geo. H. Neely, John S. Chambers J. Hervey Crawford, Robt. Stringfellow, Jas. F. Wherry, Edwin Mil[illegible]

May 14th 1799

Mr John B. Davies was on this day ordained by the Presbytery of South Carolina, to the whole of the gospel ministry, and installed as the Pastor of Fishing-creek and Richardson congregations

It was unanimously agreed that Thomas Latta act as clerk for this Session, and that a record of the transactions of the same be kept; and that other papers be preserved.

N.B. The members of this Session are Samuel Neely, David Carr, David Neely, Thomas Neely and Thomas Latta.

The only papers now to be found in the hands of this Session are 1. A certificate signed by Hugh Brooke VDM, of Burt Ireland stating that Sarah Porter is a member of the church & dismissed in good standing
2 A certificate stating that William Brown & Wife Jane, Charles & Archibald his Sons, also Will. Thom & his Wife were of fair and good standing when dismissed Signed by Rev. John Lawson & William Allen. &
3 A certificate from Rev. Saml W Yongue Pastor of Lebanon recommending as in good standing Thomas Wright & Nancy his Wife—

The following is a register of the Communicants in Fishing-creek at this date. viz

John B. Davies Pastor

Polly Davies	Thomas Wright	Sarah Boyd
Samuel Neely (Elders)	Agnes Wright	Christopher Strait
David Carr (Elders)	Wm Anderson	Rose Strait
David Neely (Elders)	Joseph Walker	John Mills
Thomas Neely (Elders)	Wid. Bishop	Sarah Gill
Thomas Latta (Elders)	Wid. McCulloch	Josiah Porter
Sarah Neely	Mary Elliott	Rachel Porter
Margaret Carr	Jas. Armstrong	Total 48.
Agnes Neely	Jane Armstrong	Received on examination in 1799.
Prudence Neely	Charles Brown	
Martha Latta	William Thom	Elizabeth Mills
John Latta	Agnes Thom	Elizabeth Neely
Margaret Latta	John Walker	Isabel Allen
Eliz. Chambers	Martha Walker	Sarah McHugh
Wid. McClure	Jane Walker	... on certificate
Martha Gaston	Elizab. Leman	Thomas Miller
Hugh McClure	Wid. Knox	Making a total of
Jane McClure	David Boyd	53 Members.
Mary Porter	Margaret Boyd	
David Davis		
Jane Davis		

6/ Baptisms in 1799

May 19	Geo. Gill	Sarah Duncan	Jun 30.	Jon. Jones	Janet Simpson
	Mrs G. Stuart	Mary	Aug. 11	Rob. Smith	{ William Cooper Narcissa
	Will. Walker	James		Geo Kelsey	Robert
	Jas. Gill	John		Rob. Neely	Simpson
	W. Armstrong	John	Sept. 8	Wm Whiteside	- - - -
Jun 16	Jas. Neely	Jane	28	Agnes Jenkins	William
	Thos. Gill	Archibald	Nov. 17	Jno. Anderson	Robert Reid
	Jos. Neely	Naomi Reimer	Dec 1	Kim. Duncan	- - - -
	David Davis	Jane		Charles Boyles	Martin

Total 19 Infants-

Communicants admitted in 1800

On Examination Joseph Neely, Margaret Neely, Robert Neely, Margaret Neely, Benj. Dunlap, Jane Dunlap Thomas Gill, & Agnes Gill — 8 — Wid Knox died 1

Making 53+8−1=60 & Baptized 22 Infants viz

Mar. 23	Josiah Porter	. Thomas	Jul 13	D. McCants	William Harmon
May 4	Hugh McClure	. Hugh		Philip Fox	Eleanor Gill
	Chs Brown	. William	27	Will. Boyd	John Porter
Jun 15	Mrs J. Stuart	. Darius	Aug 21	Jas. Arthur	Margaret
29	And. Stinson	. Andrew	24	Jane Neely	Viney
		Elizabeth	Oct 19	Jas. Neely	Thomas Carson
		. Abigail		P. Hamilton	Tassus
		Joseph		W. Chambers	Wm. Absalom
July 13	And. Whitney:	Leonard		Agnes Jenkins	Thadeus Freshwater

Nov 2	And. Neely	John	Nov. 30	Thos. Wright	James Reed
16	Jno. Silleman	James	Dec 14	Benj. Dunlap	Agnes Neely

June 15. 1800

This day Mr Andrew Stinson late of the covenanting Church, and a residenter in the bounds of this congregation for some time past produced Certificates and expressed his desire to be admitted a member of this church. One of these papers represented him as being from Clogh in Ireland in 1771 and stated that he (A Stins was then a single man and had from his infancy lived in that congregation - that he had always behaved himself soberly and inoffensively, free from public scandal - and that as his intention was to remove to America, he might be safely received into any Christian congregation, signed Joseph Douglas VDM & W Edmondson S clk The other was a pass given on his removal from Pennsylvania, which represented him as a sober young man free from any incumbrance or debt. . . . .
Whereupon the Session taking these papers under consideration, and inasmuch as to their own knowledge the said A. Stinson, has lived in the bounds

of this congregation nearly seven years; and to the best of their knowledge supported a sober and inoffensive conduct, it was therefore the unanimous opinion of the Session that he be received as a member of this Society—that he become subject to the rules of this Church and be admitted, when convenient to the privileges of the church

Mr Davies' January 8th 1801

The Church of Fishing=creek met at the call of the Moderator. Present Rev J.B. Davies, Moderator Elders, David Carr, David Neely, Thomas Neely & Thomas Latta together with the corresponding member from Richardson viz Walter Brown, Jas. Crawford James Gaston, Isaac McFadden, Joseph Gaston and Felix Davies— Constituted with prayer.

The Moderator informed the Session of the reasons for calling this meeting of the Session as follows That some time past a complaint was lodged by David Carr a member of Session at the instance of public Fame, that Agness Carr the wife of Robert Carr had probably been guilty of the crime of Intoxication at her own house on a Lord's day morning in February last, and at sundry other place at other times — and that the said charge was to be supported by the testimony of Martha Latta, Margaret Carr, John Thompson, John Millar & James McCammon — And he submitted the matter to the Session, whe: the crime alledged meritted investigation. The Session deemed it to be of such a nature as to call for a serious attention and so agreed to take it under consideration for trial.

The Moderator informed Session that he had by virtue of the power vested in him by the Constitution of the Church issued orders to the Clerk to Cite the accused together with the requisite Witnesses: which order upon enquiry appeared to have been complied with. and several of them, together with the accused were present.

x Messrs Carr, Latta & J. Nely for certain reasons which were suggested, requested to be excused from sitting as judges in this trial Excused —

Mrs Agnes Carr was called on — the charge was read to her and enquiry made whether she plead guilty or not guilty. She, to the enquiry plead, by confessing that at certain other times she had taken more than was for her good, yet as to the time she is specially charged in February last she pleads not guilty. She was solemnly dealt with, if guilty, to make confession, but she still persisted in pleading not guilty.

Ordered that Session proceed to the trial of this case, she being ready.

Martha Salla, being duly sworn deposeth that on a certain sabbath morning in February last she went down with some persons who were moving to the State of Georgia, to Robert Carr's where a part of the company and their Waggons were stopped —that when she went into the house, Nancy went took a bottle of Whiskey off the Shelf, held it to her head as tho' she drank, and handed about a=mong the company—she then sat down, and allow=ed that it would not do for the people to set out that morning, it was so bad and late. She also ob=served that they had fine breakfast &c I saw as I thought that she had been drinking—that after=wards, Mr Ramsey came in—brought his bottle—

1

She drank and gave the children some — that the people began to gather up their affairs — Mr McCain handed about his bottle — she drank again; which was the third time I saw her drink — That after the bottle was handed about the third time She or Nancy sat down upon a chair before the fire — She put her hand behind upon her haunch and talked some time — She observed she was sick — her head began to hang to the one side — the tears to run from her eyes. [illegible] from her [illegible] We (Mrs Ramsey & myself) wished her to go to bed — she would not. When we could not get her to go to bed we let her alone — Her head turned to the other side and hung down — She got up and said she would go nigh the fire — She went towards the jam. In turning about the chimney she fell, but raised herself so as to set against the jam & said she was getting sick. I then went out with Mrs Ramsey and staid out until word was sent out for Mrs Ramsey to come in — She went and called me in. I went and Nancy was stretched on the hearth, with only her head leaning on the jam Mrs Ramsey told me to bring a petty coat, for the woman was in a bad way on the cold hearth — and

Talked that she was going to miscarry—and said that Nancy told, her, that her child was dead—She roll. ed and tumbled about and would not be held by us. —That John Ramsey came in why not put the woman to bed—He caught hold of her and held her up, & we put a coverlet under her— Mrs Ramsey said we must get some tansey for her, it was good for her let what might ail her. Nancy was asked if there was any there. She said she did not know, ask Robin I sent home for some—We got her to bed—I was asked if I would stay till Robin would convey the Waggons beyond The Black Jacks—(They had attempted to start but their horses would not pull) I refused to stay by my-self—Robin then went for Mrs Carr. During the time Nancy threw herself about in the bed—I observed, she would hurt herself and baby too. She replyed, pla-guy fear, and the like expressions. That after Robin brought Mrs Carr he drove off the Waggon. After this she again began to toss about, and to cry out, her child was dead, and had been for four weeks, and that we would not do any thing for her—We sent after Robin being affrighted at her saying her child was dead and had been so, so long - That afterwards we carried her to the fire and sat her on a chair, but she would not sit and would fall down either to the one side or the other of the chair. And when we would say that she would hurt herself she would reply plaguy fears &c - That after we kept her as long upon the chair as we could, we took her to bed again. This being done, it was said that Andrew Letsinger & Alexr. Craig were coming. It was obser by some of us in the house, that it was not common for men to be where sick women were. I said that there was not any thing to prevent any body coming in. Nancy heard and said her brother Alexander should come. She called him to her and told him she wanted her mother. She also told A. Letsinger something about a bottle (but I could not hear distinctly what) He however got a bottle, and I expected he was going for Whiskey, and observed that we wanted no more there - I asked what he was going to do with the bottle, & he answered he was going for some whiskey. I told him no. We had had too much that morning already, & told to go with A. Craig for his mother & took the bottle from him - Several times after they went away Nancy asked

asked if Andy was come back with the Whiskey — That she appeared to have pains; but I could not think that they were proper labor pains, & were very unlike to any I had ever seen her have. Agreeably to Mrs Ramseys instructions we gave her plenty of Tansey tea. She drank as well as I remember the most of three tinfull's — that she desired to be out of the bed — We at refused to let her up but at last consented, took her & placed her on a chair at the fire. We asked her if she felt any thing like what she did when she miscarried before and she replied, no plaguy bit &c We again took her to bed, but she would not stay & so we had to take her back that by this time she became able to sit without hanging her head, yet discovered to have pains — After she sat here some time she caught Mrs Carr & said, Mother I'll shake you limb from limb — I'll leave you limbless and that some time after this Mrs Gaston came; at which time Nancy had gotten considerably better

Question by the Sesson: How long do you suppose it was from the time, the bottle went round until Mrs Gaston came? It was as I thought a good while — the Waggoners had to geer their horses — attempted to start, but their horses re=

refusing to pull, they requested the assistance of Robin. He then went for Mrs Carr & brought her, started the Waggons and brought Mrs Gaston, which took some considerable time. I don't recollect what time of the day it was when Mrs Gaston came; but the sun was so high that the ice had mostly fallen from the trees and the people thought that it would be scarcely worth while loosing out to feed till night when they started. Approved by the Witness.

Margaret Carr being duly sworn deposeth That she was there a part of that day on which the aforesaid A. Carr is charged with the crime of intoxication — that when she went Nancy was in the bed, that she spoke to her — and turned from her to the door where Mrs Latta was standing, and said she thought that Nancy had too much liquor — she thought she smelt very strong of it — that after Nancy had lien and tossed on the bed & we endeavored to hold her still (it required us both to do it) she would raise herself & say that her child was dead. We asked her if she thought it was dead — she replied she thought it was and had been four weeks. She still continued to toss and throw herself about on the bed. I observed if her child was not dead, she would kill it: to which she replied, no danger plaguy fears—That Nancy wanted to be at the fire & we helped her there, put her on the chair & held her there—that there was a cup of Tansey boiling on the fire when she first went in—that they boiled two more and gave of it to her very frequently to drink, until Mrs Gaston came—that before Mrs Gaston came she had gotten some better—this we discovered from her being able to talk & sit better. Being enquired at, she supposes that it might be about 12 O'clock when Mrs Gaston came—As to the coming of A Bray & A Sitsinger she deposes similar to what Mrs Dalla had done.

Questions by Mrs A. Carr—Was it not said by you that you thought if I had a little liquor stewed up with some tansey that it would remove the pains I had? Ans. I said no such thing. Did you not say that you thought my pains were the worst you had ever seen me have? Ans. I said I thought the maddest I ever saw.

Approved by the Witness

The testimony introduced by the church closed.

Witnesses introduced by the Defendant—

Thomas Miller being duly sworn deposes

That he happened to be at Mr Carr's that sabbath on

Agnes Carr is charged with intoxication the sun not being an hour high—that he went to the bed side where she was lying (understanding she was unwell) he asked her what was the matter with her—she said she had been helping a woman to lift a pot—that the woman let the hooks go too soon, and that in consequence of the weight of the pot she had received a hurt, and was afraid she was about to loose her little one—He being asked, says he believe she had been up for her clothes were on, and that he could not discover any sign of her being in liquor. Approved by Witness

Andrew Letsinger being duly qualified deposes that A. Craig and himself were passing by on their road home, that they went in, that Nancey appeared to be in great pain; that she wanted A. Craig to go for her mother; that he consented to go; that some of them, but remember who, wanted him to go for some whiskey, and that they gave him a bottle; that A. Craig desired him to go with him—and that he did not know whether was any whiskey there or not, for he neither saw nor smelt any. He being asked says, that he does not remember that Mrs Latta told him that they had had whiskey enough already that morning.

Approved by the witness

18 Alexander Craig being duly sworn deposes That on the Sabbath before mentioned. He was at Robert Carrs with A. Letsinger — that he saw no appearance of liquor — Nancy was in the bed and appeared to be very bad — He went to the bedside, leaned down & spoke to her but smelt nothing like liquor — that this was as nearly as he can recollect about 9 or 10 O'clock — that after he spoke to he turned round to Mrs Carr who told him that he must go for his mother & he agreed to go — and that she also told him that Nancy was very bad in labor — that afterwards she told one of us that we must go to Mr Key's for some liquor — that he said to Mrs Carr it would be better to let the liquor stand until he would return from his fathers or until Robert would come & he could go. Being asked, he says, that he does not remember any thing about the bottle being given to A. Letsinger, he being out after his mare. Appd. by Witness

Martha Gaston being duly sworn deposes The she that morning went to Robert Carrs as near as she can guess between 10 & 11 O'clock; but saw nothing either in words or actions in Nancy which discovered her to be in liquor — saw nothing about her ex-

extraordinary, but her stretching, which she considered as being occasioned by unnatural labor, which on examination she had reason to believe she was distressed with – That she thought once she smelt liquor but from what conversation she had with her, she could not think that she was injured by it. Question to Mrs Gaston – How long after this was it that she fell asleep? Ans. Some time about dusk. Approved by the Witness

The testimony here closes –.

The Session having seriously, deliberately & maturely considered the testimony adduced in the above case do find the above named Agnes Carr to have been guilty of the crime of Intoxication. And Session do therefore Judge that she be suspended from the privileges of the Church until she confess her guilt, and profess her repentance before the Church Session –

The above minute was then read to the said Agnes Carr and she was interrogated whether she submitted to the said judgment or appealed to a superior Judicatory. To this she felt unwilling to reply. Indulgence was therefore given for four weeks when she was requested to make her will known to the Moderator. Adjd. with prayer J.B. Davies Mod.–

The Session being met July 12th 1801

The Moderator reported that having lately called on to preside in Purity Session Mr Hugh Gaston, lay-elder, lately of that congregation applied for a dismission from them to join this church and obtained it. And the moderator was directed to report that Mr Gaston was in regular standing and might be received as such. Accordingly he was admitted to membership with us. He was also chosen consented and appointed to act as a ruling elder in this congregation.

The Session being met July 26th 1801

Mr Andrew Kennedy late of Ebenezer congregation produced a certificate of his having received privileges and recommending him for admission elsewhere
Signed Jan 21st 1801 Wm Atkins Elder

The Session being convened October 21st 1801

Mr John Barr wishing to be connected with this Church produced a certificate from Rev Jo. Dawson in Ireland dated Sept. 28th 1792 of freedom from public scandal or church censure & as he has resided in this congregation, he was considered as prepared to be admitted, provided he give evidence of piety-

Baptised up to October

Feb. 22	Wm Walker	Matilda	Jul. 26	Abr Whiteside	Will. Jones
Mar 8	Jos. Neely	Polly		And. Kennedy	Eliza Jane Priscilla Elizab.
	Jas. Gill	Nathan	Sep 6	Jno Neely	Mary
22	John Harper	Sarah		Leonard Jones	Alex. Pagan
	Chs. Boyles	Margaret		Abr. Gill	Lucinda
Ap 30	W. Armstrong	Eleanor		Mr Js Kraet	Mary Cooper
May 2	Jn. Hardin	John Seely	20	Wm Neely of S.	John
17	Wm Gill	Jonathan		Thomas Miller	John Litringer
Jun 14	Jn. Workman	Robert Patton		Eliz. Mills	Hugh
28	Alex. McGahie	Jane		Will. Johnston	Elizab. Patterson
Jul. 12	Jas. Hemphill	Jas. Bratton		22 Infants.	

Communicants admitted in 1801 } 60+13+4−2−6−1=68

On Examination William Walker, Margt. Gill of Geo. Mary Poage Elizabeth Brown, John Anderson ... Anderson, Jane Walker jun James Neely, Mary Leman, Elizabeth Latta Abram Whiteside, Jane Whiteside, Sarah Johnston — 13

On Certificate — Jane Neely, James Arthur, Hugh Gaston, Martha Gaston. 4

Died — Wid. McClure, Elizabeth Leman — — 2

Dismissed. Jno Mills, Eliz. Mills, Jos. Neely, Margt. Neely Benj. Dunlap, Jane Dunlap — — — — 6

Suspended — — David Carr - - - - - - - -

Session being convened Jany 24th 1802
Alexander McGahie from Bethesda produced a certificate signed by John Murphy, Elder stating that he had received priviledges & his character was good. He was received.

Session being convened May 30th 1802
Daniel Cook produced a letter from a Society in Kershaw District relative to Delfey his wife, formerly Reese stating that she had been received to the priviledge of baptism for her child. She was examined as to her religious knowledge and religious experience as well as ~~cook~~ that of Mr Cook. & receiving satisfaction, they were admitted to enjoy the privilege of Baptism for their children

Baptised from October 1801 to Dec. 31. 1803

Oct. 18	Jno Anderson	Becky Gragg	Mar 21	J. Chambers	Elizabeth
	Jon. Jones	Sarah Garner	May 16	A Neely	Elizabeth
	Jno. Barr	Mary Barkley	30	Joseah Porter	Joseah
Nov. 1	S. Lowrey	Jn. Drayton		Dan. Cook	Mary Janet
	W. Thorn	Charles		A Whurry	Mary Stuart
15	Rob. Neely	Thos. McCulloch	Jun 13	Thos. Davis	John
	Jno Burns	Jane Henry		Mrs J. Stuart	-- -
Dec 13	Chs. Brown	Nancy Anne		Jno. Porter	Mary
27	S. Mahood	Martha Lusk	Sep 5	Geo. Gile	Christian Stuart
1802 Jan 24	W. Whiteside	Joseph Jones		Phil. Fox	Jenny
Feb 7	Jas. White	Jane Martin		Jas. Gill	John
				Jno Harper	Margt. Miller

24 Infants

Communicants' Register for 1802

Received on examination James & Mary Gill, John Gill Elizabeth Gill, George Gill, James H. Walker, Abram Gill Agnes Gill, Mary Porter, Andrew Kennedy, Thomas Porter Agnes Boyd, Elizabeth Neely of T. Florah B. Porter, Priscel la Buford, Andrew Bradford, John Neely, Mary Neely John Porter, Sarah Porter, Charles Boyd, Will. Hamilton Elizabeth Porter & D. Carr, restored 24

Died - - Hugh McClure, John Walker 2

Dismissed. Elizabeth Neely of D. Isabel Allen, Eliz. Latta William Hamilton, David Carr, Margt. Carr, Eliz. Cham= bers, Thomas Wright, Agnes Wright, W. Anderson, David Neely, Agnes Neely, David Boyd, Margt. Boyd Christopher Strait, Rose Strait. Thomas Miller, Abram Whiteside, Jane Whiteside, Sarah Johnston, Jno. Anderson Mrs Anderson, Jane Walker & Jas. Arthur 24

Suspended, Martha Walker (68+24-21=24-1=65) 1

Session being convened May 29. 1803

James Means jun produced a certificate under the hand of the Rev W. Williamson of Fair-forest stat ing that he was a young man of fair moral charac ter & in full communion. He was received to member ship

Baptized in 1803

Date	Parent	Child
Feb. 27	David Davis	Mary
Mar 13	K. Banian	Marg^t. Eliza
Ap 10	J. H. Walker	Jane Henry
	Will. Boyd	Hugh McClure
	Will Walker	William
17	Jno. Harden	Peter
	Jane Hopkins	Elizabeth Taylor
May 29	Thos. Miller	Eliz. Hendman
	Saml. Mahood	Agnes
	Jno Gill of Rb	Thomas Walls
Jul. 3	Thos. Lalla	Thomas
		Sarah Ferguson
17	Jas. Walles	Melinda
	Will Bradford	Margaret
	Will. Clinton	Elizabeth
		W^m. Elliott
		James

Total 17. Infants.

Communicants' Register. Received
On Examination Elizabeth McCulloch, Anne Porter
Samuel Mahood, Jane McCormick, Elizab. T. Davis 5
On Certificate James Means, William Cunningham 2
Died Samuel Neely, Elder James H. Walker 2
Dismissed, Widow McCulloch, Mary Elliott 2
As per last year 65+5+2−2−2 = 68 Total

September 5 1804 Messrs Josiah Porter, William Walker, Charles Brown & David Davis were ordained Elders in this congregation

Register of Communicants received 1804
On examination Susan Miller, Mary Gill of T. Wid Nelson
Elizabeth Armstrong, Agnes Mahood, James Bradford
Eleanor Gill, John Gaston of H. 8. On Certificate James Steele, Mary Steele
Sam. Lewis, James Wallis Sarah Wallis − 5 Total 13

Dismissed. Joseph Walker, Priscilla Buford & W. Cunningham 3

Suspended. Thomas Porter 1

As per last report 68+8+5−3−1 = 77 Total

Baptized in 1804

Date	Parent	Child	Date	Parent	Child
Apr 3	Jno B. Davies	Frances Janet	Oct 21	James Gill	Martha Heddleson
Jul 15	Will. Thom	Margaret		Will. Boyd	Milton
Aug 5	Chs. Brown	Mary	26	Jno Harper	...Eleanor
19	Saml Gill	Hugh McClure		And. Wherry	Willis
Oct 1	John Neely	....		Charles Boyles	...... Total 10 Infts

Register communicants received 1805

On Examination, Philip Fox, Mary Fox, William Boyd, Keziah Boyd, Mrs Jones & Rose a Black woman 6

On Certificate, Mary Smith, James E. McFadden, Susan McFadden 3

Died James Neely 1

Dismissed Wid Bishop, James Means & Susan Miller 3

As per last 77+6+3−1−3 = 82 Total

Baptized in 1805

Date	Parent	Child	Date	Parent	Child
Feb. 10	And Bradford	Thos. Neely	May 19	Jo Whiteside	Jonathan
				Jno Gill of K	Eleanor Downing
24	Will Walker	Eliza	Dec 8	J.E. McFadden	Polly Buford
	Sam Mahood	Mary		David Davis	Lythia Harlan
Mar 10	Jas. Neely of R	Anne			John Latta
Apr 22	Jas Steele	Margaret			
May 19	W. Armstrong	Jonathan		Total	11 Infants

Register of Communicants 1806. Received On Examination. Sarah Neely of T. Sarah Banian Martha Walker, restored

On Certificate, Mary Bradford, John Wright --- Wright and Lettice Hamilton 4

Dismissed, Will Thom, Agnes Thom, Will. Walker, Jane Walker, Sarah M Hugh, A. Kennedy, Jas. Bradford, Eliz. Bradford, John Gaston & Rose a blk woman 10

Suspended Anne P. Gaston.

As last report 82+3+4—10—1 = 78 Total

Baptized in 1806

Jan 26	Jas Walles	Franky Carolin	May 3	Chs. Boyles	Jas Neal
Mar 9	D. Cook	Delila Campbell		Ph. Fox	Susan. Grove
30	Ch. Brown	Archibald	Aug 10	Peter Boyd	Mary Cooper
Sept 13	Jno. Gill (R.G.)	Jno. Marshall		J Hamilton	John
	Sam. Gill	Jno. Alexander		Total	9 Infants

Register of Communicants 1807 to March 1808

On examination. Mary Gill of S. Marg. Carr, readmitted, Jno Neely 3. Rachel Neely, John Boyd. Mrs D. Boyd, Mrs R. Gill Esther Buford Patience Stringfellow 6

Died Sarah Neely, David Davis, Mrs D. Boyd Thos. Latta.. 4

Dismissed Jno Porter, Sarah Porter, Rob. Neely Margt. Neely and Mary Porter of T. 5 As per last Report 78+3+6—4—5 = 78

Baptized from Oct. 1806 until April 1808

Oct 7.	Sam. Lewis.	Smith Leman	Aug 30	D. Boyd of J.	Janet Gill
Nov 9	A. Bradford.	Rob. McCartney	Nov. 1	Rob. Gill	Agnes
1807 Jan 11	Will. Boyd	Will. Harvey	14	Jno Neely of J.	George Harvey
May 17	Will Clinton	Anne Neely Sarah Elliott	15	Jno Boyd of R	Mary Adelite
Jun 7.	Jas Gill Sen.	Robert	Dec 13	Jon. Wallis	William Dunlap Thos Lysander
14.	Dan Cook.	Martha Neely	1808		Polly Teresa
	Jno Wright	Jno Randolph	Feb. 14	Jno Neely Sen	Agnes
Jul. 5.	And Whiry	Silas	17	Will. Gaston Pat. Shingfellow	LeRoy Buford Jas Madison
	Alex Pagan	John Mills		Esther Buford	Jefferson
29.	Jon Jones	Anne Jonathan	28	J. E. McFadden	Isaac
Augt 9.	Sam McKnoo	James		Total 25 Infants	

June 1st 1808

Messrs Charles Boyd, James Steele James Walles & Samuel Lewis were set apart to the office of Ruling Elder in this congregation.

Register of Communicants to March 1809. Received On examination Samuel Neely, Mary Neely, Wm Whiteside Jenny Porter, Juliett G. Porter & John Boyd Sen 6.

Died Lettice Hamilton, Thomas Gill, Margt Gill, J Boyd S. 4

Dismissed John Gill

As per last report 78 + 6 − 4 − 1 = 79. Total –

Baptized from March 1808 To March 1809

Apr 3	Wm. Jane Davies	Margaret	Aug. 31	Jos. Boyd	Mary anne
					Lee
	Ch Brown	Jn Lewson Davies			Joseph
10	Jon Jones	Jn Downing	Sept. 3	Jenny Porter	4 Adults
Jun 6	Eliza. Gill	Robert Harvey		Juliette G. Porter	
Aug 14	Chs. Boyles	Hugh Collins	Oct 2	Philip Fox	William
			Nov 6	Will. Clinton	Jno Penchon(?)
28	Peter Boyd	Nancy		Jas. Armstrong	Agnes
31	Sarah Boyd	an Adult	Dec 4	Will. Boyd	Susan. Eliza
					3 Adults & 13 Infts

Register of Communicants from March 1809 to 1810

On Examination, John R. Buford, David Boyd Mary Boyd
Mary Garton 4

Dismissed McGill, Robinson, Eliz. Gill, Mary Bradford 3

Suspended George Gill 1

Last report 79 + 4 − 4 = 79

Baptized from March 1809 to March 1810

Mar 12	Sam Lewis	Will. Linn	Jun 25	Alex Pagan	James
	Jas. Gill - -	Agnes Jenkins	Aug 6	S. Mahood	Hugh
26	Saml. Neely	David Davis	Sept 17	Will. Walker [illegible]	Mary Boyd
May 7	Jas. Walker - -	Jas. LeRoy	23	W. Armstrong	Jefsa(?)
	Geo Gill KS	Nancy	Nov 5	John Neely, J.	Prudence Selina
22	Peter Wylie	William	19	William Elliott	Sally Minerva
28	Jas. Elliott	Mary Boyd	1810 Jan 14	J.R. Buford	Deidamia
Jun 25	Dan. Cook	Daniel Reese		P. Stringfellow	Catharine Elvira
	Sam Gill	Joana Elvira		Total	17 Infants

Register for 1810 — ~~1811~~ to April 1811

Communicants received on Examination

Hannah Wherry, Joseph Boyd, Sarah Boyd, Alexr. Gaston and William Nelson 5

On Certificate, Agnes Porter, Agnes McElhenny, Margt. Chambers 3

Dismissed, Chs Brown, Eliz. Brown, John Neely & Mary Neely 4

Last report 79+5+3−4 = 83.

Baptized from March 1810 to Apr. 1811

Mar 17	Alex Gaston	Jinsey Douglas	Aug 25	J B Davies (KBW	Louisa Susanah
Ap 8	And. Wherry	Peggy	Sep 9	W Bradford	Mary Julilah
	Jno Thompson	Christ. Strait	19	John Thompson	John Mills
May 13	Jos. Boyd	Jinsey Clarke			Rachel
	Rob. Gill	Harriett			
	James Gill	Elizab. Porter	23	John Boyd	Jas. Mad. Neely
Jun 2	R McElhenny	Harriet Minerva	Nov 19	David Boyd	Hugh Gaston
	A Bradford	Sarah Teressa		Will. Boyd	Mary Keziah
Jul 8	Jas. Strait	John	1811		
		James	Jan 13	Chs. Boyd (E)	Mary
	Peter Boyd	Betsey Ferguson	Mar 10	Sam. Lewis	Jas. Alexander
	Rob. McFadden	Polly Steele	24	Sam. Gill	Eleanor
	Peter Wylie	Peggy Steele		Geo Gill BS	John
	Jas. Armstrong	Jas. Stewart			

Total 25 Infants.

Register from April 1811 to April 1812, Received On examination, John Chambers, Robert McFadden Sarah McFadden, Sarah Latta, William Porter, William Smith, & George Gill restored

On Certificate, William McDaniel, Jane McDaniel, Sarah Smith 3.

Died, James Steele, Elder 1

Dismissed, Sarah Gill, James Gill, Mary Gill, Mary Fox, William Whiteside 5

Suspended, Philip Fox.- (last report 83+7+3-1-5-1=86)!

Baptized from Apr 1. 1811 to Apr 1812.

Date	Parent	Child	Date	Parent	Child
1811 Jun 8	William Smith, an adult		Nov. 10	Peter Wylie	John
				Jos. Steele - -	Polly
	Geo Gill Col	Greenberry	Dec 8	Alex. Lewis	Will Rainy
	Wid McFadden	Wm Downing John	1812 Mar 1	S. Mahood - -	Isabella
17	Chs Miller C.P.	John McBride	15	J R Buford	Jemima Susanah
Jul 21	Jas Waller - -	Will. Garvey		Will. McDaniel	Mary Martha
Aug 4	Will. Clinton	Thos Newton White		R McFadden	Sally Caroline
	Alex Pagan	Thos Sumpter		Alex. Gaston	Martha Matilda
	D. Bradford P.	Mary Anne	29	Dan. Cook	Neel McDonald
Nov 10	Will. Elliott	John Enos			
	John Thompson	Sarah Linn Patsey		1 Adult & 21	Infants

May 30 1812 Messrs James E McFadden & John Boyd were set apart to the office of ruling Elder in the room of James Steele deceased & Charles Brown dismissed

Communicants' Register from April 1812 to Ap. 1813

On examination Will. Jones, Wid. Downing, readmitted - 2

On Certificate, Jas Boyd, Marg.t Boyd, Esley Nelson 3

Died Eleanor Gill, Barr=1 } Last report 86+2+3-1= 90.

Baptized from Apr 1812 to Apr 1813

Jun 28	Mrs Champion	Cynthia	Oct 11	Jno Boyd Elder	Rachel Amanda
Aug 2	P. Stringfellow	Robert Henry	25	Peter Boyd	Jno. Anderson
	Jos. Boyd	Eloisa Lavinia		Mrs J. Wylie	Zorah Camack
11	Jas Boyd	William Lewis			Janet Bell
	R. McElhenny	- - - - - -			
Sep 20	Rob. Gill	Effy	Dec 6	David Boyd	Marg. Caroline
	Jno. Kelsey	Betsy Matilda.	1813 Mar 21	Will. Nelson	George
				Total 13. Infants —	

Register Communicants from Ap. 1813 to Ap. 1814 recd.

On examination, Charles Boyd jun, Elizab. Latta Fred. Davis 3

On certificate, Mary Bradford, Mary Porter of S. 2

Dismissed, Jos. Porter, Rach. Porter, Mary Porter, Eliz. Porter

Jos Boyd & Sarah Boyd 6

Last Report 90+3+2−6 = 89 Total

Baptized in the same period 16 Infants viz

Ap 5	Saml Gill	Jas. Newton	Dec 9	Thos. Whele	Thos. Ancrum
	Ch. Boyd	Anderson McKinny			Nathan Neely
	Will. Elliott	James Harvey			James
25	James Gill	Lewis Harrison			Elizabeth
	A. Whery - -	William			Margaret
	Jno Neely	Thomas Amzi			William
Jun 20	Sam. Lewis	Jenny Narcissa	0	Felix Davy	Eliz. Brown
	R. McFadden	Eliza Matilda			James

May 30 1812

The Session being convened, Robert B. Porter and Mary his wife voluntarily presented themselves before the Session, and professed their penitence on account of the crime of fornication & were received as members — Mr Porter was baptised —

Register, of Communicants received from Ap 1814 to Ap 1815

On examination, Eliz. Boyd of Jn Marg^t Boyd, Thomas Eaves Polly Eaves Jenny Fox, Mary Pagan, James Gill Eleanor Gill Robert B. Porter & Mary Porter 10

On Certificate Felix Davis, Jane Davis, Henry Fox, and Jenny Kennedy 4

Dismissed, Henry Fox, Jenny Fox 2

Last report 89 + 10 + 4 − 2 = 101 Total -

Baptized from Ap 1814 to Ap 1815 1 Adult & 28 Infants viz

Date	Parent	Child
Ap. 24	Saml Neely	Thomas Berry
May 15	Peter Wylie	Jesse
	Will Boyd	Dav. Harrison Wilds
	Will Smith	John Strong
	Geo. Gill Be	Anne
	Jos. Steele	Jas. Harvey
29	Alex Pagan	Alex. Lawrence
	John Poage	Jas. Harrison
	Will Boyd of J	David Anderson
Jun 4	Thomas Eaves	Lucy Saunders Violet Fernandes
6	Alex Gaston	Joseph Harper
	Jas Boyd	Robt. Cummins
	L. Downing	Mary
Aug 10	Robert Brookfield Porter, Adult	
Aug 20	R B Porter	Eliza
22	J R Buford	Jno. Osmond Holliday
	Pat. Stringfellow	Eliza Bella
	Will Poage	Joseph Steele
Sep 4	Mrs J Wylie	Geo. Nelson
Oct 2	And Bradford	Pandora Latta
	Will. Clenton	Thos. Fleming Polly Cath. Davis
23	Chs Boyd of C	Mary Ann Steele
	Jas. Black	Elizab. Weir
	Jas. Elliott	Betsy McCance
	R McElhenny	James
1815 Mar 12	Jas. Walles	Mary Terressa
	Will Nelson	Robt. Kennedy

John Neely was on September 30 1815 and Dr. Alexr. Rosborough on October 2d 1815 ordained Elders in this congregation

May 31st 1815 The Session being convened, Prudence Jack formerly Davids came before Session, professed her desire to be readmitted and placed in good standing in the church; accordingly after examination she made a public profession of her penitence for the crime of fornication & of her faith in Christ for pardon. Samuel Jack voluntarily joined with her in this profession and being baptized, They were admitted to church fellowship.

September 30. 1815 The Session being convened - Sarah Latta after examination and free conversation held with her came before the church and made a profession of her repentance in respect to the crime of fornication charged against her, and of her faith in the Divine Redeemer. On which she was admitted to regular standing in the Church and received baptism to her infant.

September 30-1815 John Neely was ordained an Elder in this congregation. Likewise Octob. 1st Dr Alex. Rosborough was ordained to the same office

Nov. 11. 1815 The Session being convened, Mr Philip Fox formerly a member, but who was charged by Common fame with a violation of gospel order, came before Session and voluntarily acknowledged his error and professed his sorrow and purpose of amendment. On which it was judged by the Session, that Mr Fox be absolved from the scandal & be placed in good standing, and furnished with a certificate of his standing now with us –

November 17th 1815 Thomas Neely, a member of this Congregation, died in the unshaken hope of a glorious immortality through the Redemption that is in Christ Jesus – He was also an elder in this church

Register of Communicants from Ap. 1815 to Ap. 1816 Recd.
On Examination John McFadden, Gerom Hutchinson Leander Downing, Rachel Downing, Elizabeth Boyd, Joseph Steele, Rosanah Steele, Mary Thompson, Martha Gaston Eleanor Boyd, Wm Boyd Dinah Davis, Geo. Gill Capt. Elizabeth Gill, And. Wherry, Eliz. Wherry, William Chambers Lucreha Chambers, John Latta, Jenny Latta, Jane Latta Azuba Wylie – Mrs Cooper, Mary Downing Samuel Jack John LeRoy Davies, Charles LeRoy Boyd 27

On Certificate, Dr. A. Rosborough, Robt. Miller, Jane Miller 3

Died, Abram Gill, Agnes Gill, Jane Armstrong, Thomas Neely Martha Walker 5

Dismissed Mary S. Harrel, H. Hutchinson S. Duncan C. LeR. Boyd Felix Davis & Jane Davis. 6 } Last Rept. 101+27+3–5–6=120 Total

Baptized from 1815 to 1816

Date	Parent	Child
Apr 16	I. Kelsey	Janet Sus. Mills
	Chs. Neely	Thos. Jackson Walker
May 7	Rob. McFadden	Jas. Wilson Poage
31	Samuel Jack, as an adult	
	S. Jack	William Daves
Jun 5	W. Chambers	Margt. Ros. Moore
Jul 20	Peter Boyd	Peggy
	J. H. Cooper	Robert Hamilton Leonard Stuart Peggy Belinda Jas. La Fayette
	Jon. Walker	Betsey

		--
	Alexr Barr	-----
21	Jas. Gill	John Salmonds
	R. B. Porter	Florah Terrissa
Aug 6	Rob. Gill	Elizab. Dorinda
9	Will Gilmore	Julia Terrissa
		Vicey Elvira
Aug 9	Do.	James
		Thomas Carson
	Dav. McCance	William
		James
		Robert Neely

	Will. Johnston	Hannah
	Jno Wherry	----
Sep 10	D. Downing	Rach. Clarentine
23	A. Wherry	Darky
30	Sarah Lalla	Jinsey
Nov 5	Jno Poage	Keziah Elvira
	Mary a Blk	an adult
1816 Mar 3	Jno. McFadden	Eliz Katherine
17	Will Boyd	Hugh McElree
	Saml Gill	Jane
	Thos Eaves	Nancy Murray
	Mrs Champion	William
	David Boyd	Martha Narcissa
	T. Armstrong	Jas Simpson
Ap 1	J. Boyd of R.	Will. Allen

2 Adults & 39 Infants –

Upon an inspection of the register of the summer past it will be seen that about thirty persons have been added to the communion of this church which should be recorded to the glory of the grace of God. May this work increase Transcriber

Register of Communicants from Ap 1816 to Ap 1817

On Examination, James H. Cooper Samuel Lalla

John Boyd of C, Lavina Steele, Agnes Elliott of Jas
Mary, a Blk – Charles Boyd, Sarah Boyd Jane Davis 9
On Certificate, Eliza Neely. W. Bradford Sas. Bradford 3
Dismissed Mary McFadden, John Latta Margt. Latta,
Sarah Latta, Jane Latta, W. McDaniel, Jane McDaniel,
Geo. Gill – (Last Rept. 120+9+3–8 = 124 Total) 8

Baptized from 1816 to 1817 Total 23 Infants

Ap 14	Rob. Miller	Robert LeRoy	Aug 25	Will. Elliott –	William
22	Jas. Boyd	Jno Alexander	Oct 20	Saml Neely	Will. Lemar
Jul 21	Jas. Black – –	Mary McNeil		Geo. Gill, BS	Mary
	Jas. Nelson	George	Nov 3	Dr S Rosboro'	David Decatur
	Peter Wylie	Adam Reimer		Jos. Steele	Margt. Minerva
29	Will Poage	Sarah Minerva	Dec 8	Jas. Gill – –	Octavia
	Rob. McFadden	Isaac Irwin	1817		
	Jas Shail	Margt. Matilda	Feb. 16	John Latta	Thos. Starr
Aug 11	Thos. White	Will. Clinton		Ch. Boyd of C	Margt. Elizabeth
	Mrs F. Wylie	James	Mar 16	Sam Lewis	Robert Samuel
25	John Kelsey	Will. Elliott		Alex Pagan	Geo. Bonder
	Peter Boyd	David	30	Rob. McElhenny	Jno. Addison

Register of Communicants from Ap. 1817 to Ap. 1818
On Examination, Florah Porter, Will. Neely, Lewis Gill
Mary Gill, Jane Boyd, Anne Steele, Margt Lewis, Jinsey
Millar 8
On Certificate Mary Ann Boyd, David Boyd, Mary S. Boyd
Mary McFadden Will. McDaniel, Jane McDaniel 6

Died, And. Bradford 1

Dismissed, E. McFadden, Sam. Neely. S.F. Neely, Sam. Jack

Prudence Jack 5

Suspended, Will. Jones 1

Last Report 124 + 8 + 6 − 1 − 5 − 1 = 131

Baptized from Ap 1817 to Ap 1818

Ap 20	J R Buford	Patience Emeline	Aug 3	John Poage	Hugh McClure
	Alex Gaston	Marg. Louisa	4	Will. Nelson	James
26	Florah Porter, an adult		Oct 12	W. M. Dickson	Martha Jane
	J. H. Cofer	Wm. Amberson		Will. Johnston	- - - - -
28	Jno. Neely	Lil. Alonzo	+ 26	Rob. Gill	Will. Perry
	Wid. Bradford	And. James		Will Neely	John Newton
May 18	R B Porter	Mary	1818 Jan 4	Lewis Gill	Will. Dunlap
Jun 8	Sam Latta	Rachel Emeline	Feb 8	T. Armstrong	Rebec. Edwards
	Sam. Jack	David Lawrens	Mar 8	C Boyd of D	Jacob Leander
	Will. Clinton	Eli McFadden	29	David Boyd	Will. Francis
	Will. Wylie	Sarah Lucinda			
	Lean. Downing	Ann Elmina		Total 1 Adult	22 Infants
25	Jon. Walles	Sarah Minerva			

Register Communicants from Ap. 1818 to Ap. 1819 Re-
On Examination, William Gaston, David Porter Thos. Neely
Sam. Boyd, John D. Miller, Will Jones (readmitted) Robert Buford
Will. B. Davies, Mary Mills, Margt. Stratt, Sarah Johnston,
Wm. W. Bradford, Mary Bradford, Mary Bradford jun, Jenny
Morrow, Sarah F. Latta, Eli Gill, Josiah H. Gill, Sarah Lewis
Polly Davis, Will. Linn, James Gaston, Elizabeth Wright

Jemima Wright Polly Wallis, Elias Wallis 26

On Certificate, Wid. Millan, Joseph Morrow, Jane Morrow Maryann Murphy, Will Lewis, Marg. Lewis, Edward Craw ford Jane Crawford, Ch. L R. Boyd. 9

Dismissed, J H Cooper, Mrs Cooper, Martha Latta, Jane Davis Samd Latta Eliz. Latta Dinah D. McCleary, Jane Davies jun Thomas Neely Marg. Neely Polly Davis, E. F. Latta, Wm Gaston James Wallis, Sarah Wallis, Elias Wallis 16

Last Report 131 + 26 + 9 − 16 = 150 Total

Baptized from Ap 1818 to Ap 1819

Ap	12	Jas. Boyd	James Davies	Aug 30	Thos. McFadden	Prudence Selina
		J. Armstrong	James Jackson	Oct 4	Will. Elliott	Jacob
	19	David Boyd Cc	Sarah Linney	14	Sam. Latta	Marth. Clementine
		Jas. Poage	Elizª. Rosinda	28	Dr. A Rosboro'	Florah Anne
May	3	David Porter	An Adult	Nov 15	Rob. Miller	Jas. Williamson
	24	And. Wherry	Thos. Jordan		Leand. Downing	... Simpson
		Will Jones	Jonathan LeRoy	Dec 27	Jno. McFadden	Thos. Quincy Adams
		John Latta	Peggy Anne	1819		
		Will Chambers	Elizª. Neely	Feb 28	R B Porter	James
		Jas Elliott	Dav. Fraser Boyd		Will. Jones	Will. Alexander
		Mal. Terrel	Robert		Chs Murphy	Saml. Clowney
					Will Poage	James Munro
	31	R. McFadden	Robert Buford		Will McDaniel	Sarah Agnes
Jun	16	R G Reid	James Cameron			
Jul	12	Will Smith	William			
Aug	9	W.W. Bradford	Abram Gile			

Total 1 Adult & 26 Infants

April 5 1819 Will Bradford late of Purity & Edw. Craw-ford late of Waxhaw were chosen to serve as Elders and were installed on the 24 of July 1819. It is again deemed expedient to record that under the smiles of a propitious providence and the special effusions of the Spirit of God a precious refreshing season has been witnessed in this congregation. Pleasing indications of the Divine favor was noticed in 1815. It has progressed more or less untill the present year 1819 - And about 60 members have been added to this church. In 1817 this influence has extended to the neighboring congregations of Bethesda Bethel, Bullocks creek, Salem, Beersheba & Olney -

Register Communicants from Ap 1819 to Ap 1820

On examination, William Stringfellow, Lucinda Gill Isabel F. Crawford, Lucretia Johnston, Margt Boyd of Wm Harriet Wallis, Dr Charles Boyd, Elizа Boyd, Lucey Weir Will. Poage, Jinny Poage, John Kelsey, Sarah Kelsey, James D. Crawford, Isham Kilpatrick, Mrs Cobean, John Millan Mrs Millan, John Hartness, Rachel a Blk. Patsey Do 20

On Certificate, Frances Gibbes, Narcissa Lewis 2

Died, Mary Lewis 1

Dismissed, Isham Kilpatrick, Mrs Cobean, Will. McDaniel Jill McDaniel David Boyd, Mary Boyd Lucy Weir. Wil Nelson } Suspd J Kennedy 1 - 8

40

Last Report 150 + 20 + 2 + 3 − 1 = 162

Baptized from Ap 1819 to 1820

Ap 3	William Stringfellow, Adult		Aug 22	Rachel Blk	Adult.
11	Will. Neely	Thos Latta		Rachel — —	Sidney
May 28	Ch Boyd of C	Martha Ellen	Sep 5	Peter Boyd	Jas Lawrens
	John Kelsey	Margt Anne		Jno Boyd of C	Wm Jas Lowrey
	Thos. Eaves	Jepe Thomas	Oct 18	Jos. Lewis	Mary Kez. Barnet
	Jas. Oneal	Will. Blanton	Nov 14	Jas. Black	Emeline Melly
30	Jno Poage	Sarah Lucretia	28	W. Boyd of J.	John Theodore
	Will. Wylee	Jane Kez. Porter	Dec 5	J. Whery	Mary
	Alex. Pagan	Reb. Drw. Tayjson	.	T. Whery	Wyat Alonzo
Jul 4	I K Buford	Polly McFadden	12	Lewis Gill	Geo. Wilmot
	W Stringfellow	Will. Hall	1820 Feb. 6	Jas Poage	Jno Warren
	R. McFadden	Willi Davies	+ 13	Jos M Gill	Agnes Elvy
7	Jos. Steele	Rob. Hannah	27	Will. Smith	Mary Melinda
	W M. Dickson	Jas. Steele		John Latta	Saml Neely
17	R McElhenny	Elizc. Anne			
25	Jsh. Kilpatrick	Adult		Total 4 Adults	+ 27 Infts.
	Will. S White	Do			

Register Communicants from Ap 1820 to 1821.

On Examination, John Poage, Hannah Poage, Agnes Wylee, Polly Gill of El, James Silliman, Charles Murphy James Ferguson 7

Dismissed Charles Murphy, M S. Murphy 2

Last Report 162 + 7 − 2 = 167

Baptized from Ap 1820 to Ap 1821

May 7	Peter Wylie	Peter Harvey	Aug 13	W W. Bradford	Will. Leonidas
	Jas. Boyd	Sarah Amelia	20	D A Rosboro	John Laurens
	L. Downing	Jno. Milton		Will. Wylie	Jas Alexander
20	Ch. Boyd PD	David	Sep 3	Will Poage	Rebecca Narcissa
Jun 18	Will. Nelson	Catharine	Oct 29	L Lewis	Jos. Stanhope
Jul 2	J. Armstrong	Jane Emeline	1821	Robert Miller	David
	Mat. Farrel	James	Feb 18	Sam Boyd	Jane Minerva
16	Jane Gill	An adult		Will Boyd 16	Jas Denning
	Jno Neely	John LeRoy	Mar 4	Ele Gill	Jas Laurens
	Arch Gill	Tho. Marion		Total 1 Adult + 19 Infants	
Jul 23	Anne Elliott	Betsy McCance			

Register of Communicants from Ap 1821 to Ap. 1822.

On examination, Mrs J. Strait, Darcus Strait, Mrs Hudson James Oneal, Mrs Oneal, James Poage Jenny Poage, Mary Strait ---Strait of Wid, Mrs Ferguson—Sabie, Blk, Mary A Boyd Thomas McFadden 13

On Certificate Lydia Buford, Mrs Hodges, Esther Poage 3

Dismissed Mary Bradford Eliz. W. Lott—Hannah W. Campbell Clorah P. Burns, Mrs Hodges Lewis Gill Mary Gill, Wid—Wright, Polly Wallis, Harriet Wallis, Jas Oneal, Mrs Oneal 12

Last Report 167 + 13 + 3 — 12 = 171 Total

Baptized from Ap. 1821 to 1822

Ap 3	W. Neely	Jam Clementine	Jun 2	W Johnston	Saml Harvey
May 20	Jas Oneal	Nancy Clementine	17	Rob McFadden	John
27	W Shingfellow	Harriet Davies		John Poage	Will Robinson

Jan 17	David Boyd	Jane Penniman			
Jul 8	Thomas Davis	Esther Penelope	Oct 28	A Pagan	Alexr. Robert
	J. H. Gill	Wm. Bradford	1822 Feb 4	Mr Wylie	Elvina
Aug 5	Jno. McFadden	Isaac Ewing	21	R. McElhenny	Rob. Newton
	Alex. Gaston	Jno. Alexander	Mar 3	John Latta	John Stewart
	Jno. Kilsey	Cath. Jinsey	24	J. R. Buford	Est. Amel. Carol
11	Jno. Boyd of C	Charles Lee		Ralph Harden	Mifsida Clementine
	Ralph Harden	Jno. Barr		Total 20 Infants	

Register of Communicants from 1822 to 1823

On examination, Amelia G. Davies, Louisa S. Davies

Adeline Boyd, Mary Boyd, Mary Lewis 5

On certificate Margaret Blair 1

Died, Margaret Chambers, John Boyd Senr. 2

Dismissed, Robert McFadden, Sarah McFadden,

William Linn, Agnes Elliott. 4

Last Report 171+5+1−2−4 = 171 Total

Baptized from Apr 1822 to Ap. 1823 Total 17 Infants

Ap. 7	Jas. Boyd	Rachel Elizab.	Sep 1	W. Chambers	Mary Ann Starr
	Jas. Poage	Leonard Steel	8	Will Poage	William
	Jos. Steele	Jane Black	Oct 6	Will Nelson	James
16	James Gill	Agn. Melinda Jane	Nov 17	Will Smith	Elizh. Jane
				Will Wylie	Margt. Eliza
May 19	R. McFadden	Jos. Laurens	Dec 25	Ch Boyd of C	John Workman
Jun 9	Dr. Rosborough	Jos. Brown	1823 Mar 2	Jno. Neely	David Dunlap
Jul 28	Lean Downing	Jas. Alexander		W Boyd of C	Rob. Williamson
Sep 1	Rob Buford	Sus. Almena McFadden	16	Dr. C. Boyd	Chas. Boyd (Hugh Le...)

Register of Communicants from Apr 1823 to Ap 1824

On examination, Polly B. McFadden, Hugh Gaston Samuel Woodburn, Susanah Boyd – Blacks viz David, Milley Cuffey, Esther, Willey, Ritta, Harry & Mary 12

Died, Sabio, Mary S. Boyd Sarah Boyd 3

Dismissed, Jinsey Millan, Jinsey Morrow, Jos. Morrow Jane Morrow, John Millan, Mrs Millan, Thomas Eaves Polly Eaves, Jas. Ferguson, Mrs Ferguson, Hugh Gaston, Elder Martha Gaston, Martha Gaston jun – Mary Blk Geo. Gill Elizabeth Gill, Mary Poage 17

Last Report 171 + 12 – 3 – 17 = 163 total

Baptized from Ap 1823 to Ap 1824

Ap 13	El. Gill	Jno Q. Adams	May 3	W W Bradford	Rob. De La Fayette
20	6 Blacks Adt.	David }	Aug 9	Sus. Boyd {	Jas. Williamson
		Milley } J.E. Mc		{	Mary Elizᵃ Keziah
		Cuffey }	10	2 Blks adults	Harry } Beard
					Mary }
		Willey – Knox			
		Esther – Cham	11	Sam Boyd	James Edward
		Rilla – Davies		Mel. Farrel	Thos LeRoy
21	Sam. Lewis	John Brown	Nov 23	Alex Pagan	Arch. Gill
	Will Neely	Esther Atwood			
	Jno Boyd of C	Sarah Agnes	Dec 28	J. Rosboro	Jenny Patton
	S. Woodburn	Elizᵃ Agnes		Total 8 Adults + 12 Infts.	

February 15. 1825 The Session met by the appointment of the Moderator, Constituted with prayer Present. J.B. Davies, Moderator with Elders Charles Boyd

Samuel Lewis, William Bradford, Edward Craw ford, John Boyd, Jas. E McFadden, Dr. Rosborough & John Neely. The Moderator communicated that public Rumor charged certain members of this Church as having recently been guilty of false packing of some Cotton; or of packing it so as to deceive & impose on the purchaser, which Cotton was taken to Market in November 1824. The persons against whom this charge is said to lie, are Robert Buford John R. Buford & James E. McFadden. It was judged necessary to investigate this matter.

The Moderator stated that he had given notice to the above named persons of this meeting & its object

The case of Robert Buford was first taken under consideration who appears to stand charged by Common Fame of having been engaged in false packing cotton as above stated. Robert Buford having a few days past removed to settle in the State of Tennessee does not appear. But the Moderator introduced a statement which had pro cured from the said R. Buford on this subject previous to his removal which he would submit to the Session, which was read & follows "Whereas a rumor has gotten into circulation in which I find myself implicated, as well as some others with the charge of having packed certain Cotton Bales in a way calculated to deceive and impose upon the purchaser, by which it is judged that a slander has been fixed upon the church — and whereas I am informed that the Session find it necessary to enter on an investigation of the matter I deem it my duty to make the annexed communication. Were it practicable I would freely appear in person and give the proper satisfaction. But as this is not practicable I take the liberty in this way to state the case as it is, and my views and feelings in regard to it, and leave it with to judge and act as duty may require. I do freely acknowledge that by my directions given to my servants three Bales of my own Cotton & two Bales of John R. Buford's Cotton taken to market in November 1824, was packed the good cotton on the lower and upper edge of the Bale, and Cotton of an inferior quality placed between, yet so that by an incision made on the flat side of the Bale, it would have exposed to view the inferior cotton. Now I do honestly declare to you; and through you to all others, that of this act I have been truly ashamed, and I do sin=cerely regret, that in an unguarded hour, I have yielded to the temptation, to do an act which has wounded my conscience - given occasion of grief to the serious - and opened the mouths of the enemies religion. May the Lord pardon my sin, & I hope it has taught me a lesson not to be forgotten. Signed Robert Buford"

Whereas no essential difference appears to exist between this statement, and that of common fame in regard to the said Robert Buford - Resolved That while this Session do express their decided dis-approbation of all such conduct, as a glaring vi-olation of moral obligation, and christian cha=racter, and as deservedly subjecting the perpetra-tor thereof to no small degree of censure, they judge that the said Robert Buford be admonished, and ho:ping that he is sincere in his acknowledgments and professions, that he then be considered in good stand:

ing in the church so far as this case is concerned.

The case of John R Buford inasmuch as he is necessarily absent from home, at such a distance as to preclude the practicability of his appearing before us, and has expressed his readiness to answer in this case -

Whereas James E. McFaden has been charged by public Fame as having packed a number of Bales of Cotton sold some short time previous to November 1824 in a way to deceive and impose on the purchaser, by which deed he has trespassed the laws of Christ, reproached the cause of religion opened the mouths of its enemies, and wounded the feelings of the pious, viz by packing good Cotton on the two edges of the Bale, with inferior Cotton between it - Mr McFadden voluntarily came before the Session and confessed that he had unfortunately yield to this act - that he had a load packed with good cotton on the two edges of the Bale, and inferior Cotton placed between, which he had sold in October 1824; but that in November on a discovery of the deception he had refunded to the purchaser the full price of the Cotton - that although he has un=

guardedly done the act, he never could feel approved nor has he ever attempted an apology for it- That he sincerely regrets having done it and hopes he never will be induced to repeat it. He freely acknowledges its criminality, and hopes for forgiveness through the grace of God in Christ.
After some time spent in deliberation on the confession of Mr McFadden, the Session do judge that Jas E. McFadden is guilty in this matter and that he be admonished in the presence of the Session and be retained in the Communion of the church and that he be suspended from the exercise of his office as an Elder for a season to give an opportunity to wipe off the reproach which this act has fixed on him. It was agreed that the admonition be administered to Mr McFadden next Lord's day before public worship and that our proceedings in the case be published in the Church for the satisfaction of all concerned.
The Session adjourned to meet at the Church on Sabbath morning before the hour of public worship
Concluded with prayer

The church Feb. 20. 1825 - Sabbath morning

The Session being convened and constituted - present J. B. Davies Moderator; Charles Boyd, Edw. Bradford & John Neely - Agreeably to the decision of our last meeting, an admonition was addressed to Mr J. E. McFadon and he was absolved so far as regards the church, from the scandal which his recent fall had involved, & reinstated into regular standing as a member of the church - But as the inclemency of the weather is such as has prevented a general attendance of the congregation, the publication of our proceedings in regard to this case was postponed until the first convenient opportunity - Adjourned & concluded with prayer

Note The above proceedings were published Feb. 27. 1825 -

Register of Communicants from Sp 1824 to 1825

On examination Matt. Farril Ferril, Moses. Blk - John Crocket, George Cherry, Mary. Barr, Christmas Blk Sabeo's Wife, Blk 8

On Certificate - Sarah Boyd 1

Died Jas Armstrong Le. Downing, Jno Chambers Mary Carr 4.

Dismissed - W. B. Davies C L. Boyd, S. Woodburn, A Woodburn, Jno Boyd WW Bradford. M. Bradford; J. Hartness Mrs Hartness Robert Buford

Lydia Buford, John Crockett 12

Suspended J. Silliman, C Boyd of C 2.

Last Report 163 + 8 + 1 − 4 − 12 − 2 = 154 Total

Baptized from Ap 1824 to Ap. 1825 - 1 adt 16 Infts

May 2	W. Stringfellow	Margt Jane	Jun. 25	W. S. Gibbes	Mary Caroline
	Rob Buford	Will. Maglitte	Jul 11	Jno. M'fadden	John
	Arch. Gill	Jas. Williamson		Thos. M'fadden	Saml. Newell
	Ge. Downing	William	25	Will. Boyd (C	Rach. Almena
22	Jos. Steele	Joseph White	Augt 6	John Poage	John
	Will. Jones	Jane Anne		R B Porter	Amanda Jane
23	1 Black adt	Moses Dr. B. ds	Oct 31	W. Wylie	Mary Evelina
24	J R. Buford	Jas. M'Clure	1825 Mar 20	Sam. Boyd	Robert Perrin
30	J. H. Gill - 1 -	Sarah Atwood			

May 21. 1825 The Session being convened and constituted - Present. J. B. Davies Modr. - Elders Chs. Boyd Samuel Ivers, John Boyd, Ed. Crawford Dr. A Rosborough & John Neely - Whereas a rumor has gotten into circulation, that Dr. C. Boyd a member of this church had in the latter part of the winter of the present year drank somewhat to excess, and engaged in a quarrel at Chesterville by which the interests of the church are injured and the feelings of the pious are wounded, the Doctor voluntarily appeared before the Session and tendered his acknowledgment of the fact and professed his regret on account of his fault

and his resolution through divine aid to guard more carefully against a like failure in future. The Session having considered his confession made on this occasion and having reminded him of the importance of greater watchfulness and circumspection in the Spirit of Christian charity absolve him from the Scandal incurred and do retain him in the fellowship of the church—

The case of John R Buford, who has been supposed to be engaged in fraudulently packing certain Bales of Cotton last fall appeared and stated that the Bales of Cotton alluded to in the fore named case were not thus packed either by his direction or permission— But that when it was communicated to him by the person who superintended the packing how he intended to do it, that he objected to it, alledging that it would not do—he feared it would be discovered but blamed himself because he had not positively forbid its being done so. The Moderator then introduced a written statement on the subject signed by Robert Buford stating that the aforesaid Cotton was packed by his direction in the manner specified and that when he stated to the said J. R. Buford how he had a mind to do, the said John rather objected & replied that it would not do, he feared it would be discovered or something to that effect. And further as the said John had not positively forbid him to do it, he directed it to be done so. These Statements being taken into consideration it was judged that aforesaid John R. Buford, stands acquitted of any blame in this matter, excepting so far as he refrained positively to forbid its be-ing done — and as for this neglect he has expressed his regret, and professes that was it now to be done he would decidedly and positively prohibit it.

With these statements the Session are satisfied and judge that the said J. R. Buford be retained in good standing in the church, and that in each of those cases which have been under our consideration the Session have received acknowledgments — Adjourned & concluded with prayer —

Register of Communicants from Ap 1825 to 1826.
Rec. on examination Mary D Crawford, Anne Boyd Nancy Farril & Philis, Blk 4

Died James Gaston, John D. Miller, Will Nelson
Jim McClure, Mrs Jones, Martha Gaston 6

Dismissed, J R Buford, Esther Buford Dr A Rosborough
Jenny Rosborough, Martha Stuart 5

Last Report 154 + 4 − 6 − 5 = 147 Total

Baptized from Ap 1825 to Ap. 1826 Total 1 Adt. 15 Infts

Ap 10	Eli. Gill	Rob. Walker	Aug 21	Saml Lewis	Josiah Walker
	Jas Poage	Mary Hannah		Rac. Downing	Leander
7	J. D. Crawford	Rob. Archibald	11	1 Blk adult	Phillis. Mc–
	J Kelsey	Sally Lamira	15	Jas. Boyd	Sam Williamson
30	Jno Latta	Robert ---	1826 Mar 12	Will Jones	Mary Elizabeth
Jun 5	Will. Nelson	Jane		Geo Cherry	David Alexander
	Mat Jarrel	Harvy Monroe	26	Will. Smith	LeRoy Davies +
Jul 24	Dr A Rosboro	Sam. Harvey			

Register Communicants from Ap 1826 to Ap 1827

On examination Martha N. Boyd 1

On Certificate John Boyd Margt. Boyd, Mary Bradford 3

Died Will. Bradford, Sarah Bradford 2

Dismissed. Prud. Neely, Jn McFadden Sarah McFadden
T. McFadden, Mary Mcfadden, Lucinda J Morrow, David
Porter 7

Suspended Esther, a Blk Saml. Boyd 2

Last Report 147 + 1 + 3 − 2 − 7 − 2 = 140 Total

Baptized from Ap 1826 to Ap 1827

Ap 23	Jos H. Gill	Mary Lucinda	Aug 9	Do	Florah Knox
					- - - - Knox
May 14	Alex Poage	Mary Clarke			
	W. J. Miles	Ellen Azuba	23	W. Wylie	Will. Boyd
		Mary Jane	Sep 5	Eliz. Waller	Jon. G. Osborne
28	Will. Chambers	Stuart Starr			Harriet Melinda
Jul 9	Martha Narcissa	Boyd Adelle			
	Harry (Col)	Rachel Dunlap	Dec 17	Will Boyd	Chs Leander
		Mary Crawford		El. Boyd of C	James Dunan
		Henry Crawford			
		- - Crawford	1827		
	Winny (Cn)	Mary Knox	Ap 1	Jno Lalla	James E—
		Nancy Knox		Total 1. Ad 19 Infts	

April 28th 1827 Ordained as Elders in this Church William Stringfellow, Alexander Gaston, Josiah H. Gill & installed Robert Miller

Register of Communicants from Ap 1827 to Ap 1828

On examination Cynthia Miller, Mary L. Miller Selena Ann Miller. Prud. S. Mills, Martha M. Gaston Jon Jones, W L Waller. Jane G. Waller. S McElhenny Esther McElhenny 10

On Certificate, Florah P. Burns 1

Died John Boyd, Elder, Will Chambers - - 2.

Dismissed Jno Boyd, Margt Boyd, Mary Gill, Christmas 4

Last Report 140+8+3 −2−4 = 145 Total

Baptized from April 1827 to Ap. 1828

Ap 28	Jos. Steele	James Marion	Jun 24	M. Tanel	Martha
	John Poage	Joseph Sylvanus	Jul 22	Eli Gill - -	Martha Davis
		Will. Andrew		Mary Bradford	Lucinda
May 4	Florah Burns	John David			

Jul 25	W. S. Gibbes	Octa. Theodosia	Do	Do	James
Aug 19	W. L. Wallis	David McHenry			Jinsey
	Jon Jones	Mary Anne			Thomas
Nov 11	Will Poage	Mary Jane	1828		
	David Boyd	Mary Ann Louisa	Mar 9	Jno Neely	Agnes Jane
Dec 17	Jno Watson	Adams Adt		J D Crawford	Mary Jane
	Will. Adams	Marg. Thompson			
		Will. Wylie			
		Anne Thompson		Total 1 Adt 26	Infants

Register Communicants from Ap. 1828 to Ap 1829

On examination Will. Adams, Martha Adams, Rachel Williamson, Jane Gill, Mary Boyd. Melinda Gordon, Mary a Blk restored. 7

On certificate, Mary McFadden 1

Died, Charles Boyd, Cuffey 2

Dismissed - I&K Davies, P. B. Gaston, Nancy Farrel, Hugh Gaston Samuel Lewis Narcissa Lewis 7

Suspended, W Boyd Sen, Anne Steele Dr C Boyd, Moses & Harry 5

Last Report 145+7+1-2-7-5 = 139 Total

Baptized from April 1828 to 1829 - 1 Adt & 5 Infants

Ap 00	Eliz Boyd	Charles A.	Oct 11	R B Porter	Juliet Anne
Jun 15	Will Smith	Rob. Walker	12	Melinda Gordon	adult
July 27	Will Neely	Mary Narcissa	13	Willie Wylie	. . . .
Sep 28	Arch. Gill	Mary Agnes			

Register from Ap 1829 to Ap 1830

On examination, Mary Chambers, Jinny N. Lewis, Moses Crist

Jinny - Sarah - Blk. 5

Deed William Lewis, March 3d 1830 1

Dismissed Az. Wylee, Az. McElhenny, Dav. Dickson

And Wherry Eli. Gill Polly Gill, Jas Poage - Jenny Poage 8

Last Report 139 + 5 - 1 - 8 = 135

Baptized from Ap 1829 to Ap 1830 -

Ap 27	M. Farrel	Mary Anne	Jul. 26	Will Boyd & C	Sarah Elizª
May 17	Will. Jones	Saml James	Aug 23	Jos Steele	Lavina Elizª
				Jon Jones jun	Susanah
Jun 14	Dav. Boyd	Juliet Emeline	29	W L Walles	And Jackson
	J F. Wherry	Elizª Amanda			James
28	T Calt Clure	Phebe Annie	Sep 6	Jas Poage	
			Oct 17	Jos H Gill	Margt Jane
Jul 12	Will Poage	Louisa Louisa		Sarah (Sam) Blk Adult	
	Jnº Latta	And. Jackson		Total 1 Adt. & 13 Infts	

Oct. 9 1830 At Fairforest
Approved to this date J LeRoy Davies Mod. of Bethel Py

Register of Comts from Ap 1830 to 1831

On Examination, Will. L. Lewis, Margt J. Adams, George Nel-

son, Jenny & Amy Blk C. B. 5

Deed Hannah Poage & Azuba Wylee 2

Dismissed, Mary Bradford, Geo Cherry. Margt. Cherry

John Latta, Jane Latta Sabco's Wife 6

Last Report 135 + 5 - 2 - 6 = 132 Total

Baptized from Ap 1830 to 1831 Total 2 Adts 8 Infts

Jun 20	W Wylee	Elizª Alvena	Nov 7	Dav. Boyd	Jas Alexander
	W Neely	Martha Eliza	1831 Feb 13	Ellen Boyd	Sarah Agnes
			25	Will Poage	Harriet Elizª
					Martha Parmick
July 23	W S Gibbes	Susan Adelia	Ap 3	J B Bradford	Edw. Alexr.
Oct 3	Amy & Jenny	2 Adults Ck			

Register Com^d from Ap 1831 to 1832

On Examination, Isaac McFadden, Mrs Lowrey, Eliz^a Porter
Anne Downing, Jenny Kennedy (restored) Tom Blk. A.G.
Dr C Boyd & Will. Boyd (rest^d) Rob. K. Nelson 9

Certificate Mary Poage .1

Died Eliz^a Armstrong, John Nelly (col) Mary Downing 3

Dismissed Martha M. Millar, Moses Blk Eliz. Wherry, —
Mary Thompson Rob. B Porter, Mary Porter, Eliza Porter
Juliett G. Jones, Will Jones Rac. Williamson Jane Gill 11

Suspended Willey & Jenny .2

Last Report 132 + 9 + 1 — 3 — 11 — 2 = 126 Total

Baptized from Ap 1831 to Ap 1832 Total 8 Infants

Ap 24	Will Boyd	Mary Agnes	Nov 10	M. Farrel	Eliz^a. Adeline
29	Isaac McFadden	Ja^s. McCalla	1832 Jan 22	Arch. Gill	Marth. Eliz^a.
		& Melinda Am.	Feb. 17	Jno. Poage	Samuel
May 29	J. T. Wherry	Sally Ellen	22	Lon. Jones	Eliz^a. Martha

Register Com^d from Ap. 1832 to Ap 1833

On Examination Aug. 12 Milton Boyd, Jane Boyd Jus.
E Boyd, Mary K Boyd. John W. Adams, Will W. Adams
Anne Jones Act 28 — Joseph. Poage, Marg^t Douglas, Geo
W. Neely, Thos. A Neely, David C. Crawford, Jane C Crawford
John J. Chambers, Marg^t R M. Chambers Ralph McFadden

Will P. McFadden, Rob. M. Bradford, Sarah T. Bradford Paul. L. Bradford, John Gibbes, Sarah Miller, Geo H. Miller Robt. Lek Miller, Robert H Stringfellow, Joseph H Gaston, Margt. L. Gaston, James H Poage. Nov. 11 - Robert McKorkle, Will Smith jun - - Boyd Jan 18. 1833 Will. Cowan, Margaret Cowan 33

Dismissed, Mary Chambers, Will. L. Lewis, Adel. B Bradford, Mary Downing. M. A Denning, Jon Jones Margt. Jones. Jos. H Gill Mary Gill, Mary B. Strait Mrs J. Strail Darcus S. Brown. Mrs Hudson Mrs Geo Strait Mary Strait R.H. Bradford Sarah T. Bill T.L. Bradford Mary Millar, Nancy Wylee Jenny Blk 21

Died Eliza. Bradford, Agnes Mahood 2

Suspended Ritta 1

Last report 126 + 33 - 21 - 2 - 1 = 135 Total

Baptized from Ap. 1832 to Ap. 1833

Ap 22 W. L. Wallis	Will. Lynn	1833 Jan 18	Will. Cowan	John Alexander
David Boyd	Jno Gaston			Jane
May 6 Will Neely	Sarah Eliza.			Martha
July 1 Will Boyd	John Lee			Geo Wash. Glen
29 Milton Boyd	- - - - -			Margaret
Sep 8 Jon Jones Sen	- - -			Rebec. Anne

Total 12. Infants

Register of Comts from Ap 1833 to 1834

On examination - April 14. Polly T Wherry, Clarentine Downing, Rosan. Douglas, Anderson Blk, Sep. 14th Milley & Hannah Blks 6

Died Feb. 23. 1834 Margaret Lewis

Dismissed Will. Smith, Sarah Smith, Will. Smith jun. Melinda Gordon, Sarah, Blk - James Boyd Margt Boyd Margt. D. Boyd, Robert McCorkle, Sarah McCorkle, S. McElhenny Es. McElhenny, Will L Walles J. G. Walles, Margt Douglas, Rosan Douglas Milton Boyd Jane Boyd, Anne Jones Margt. McCachran, John W. Adams 21

Last Report 135 + 6 — 1 — 21 = 119 Total

Baptized from Ap 1830 to Ap 1834

Ap 14	Anderson Blk an Adult		Jul 24	Do	Marg. Louisa
Jun 30	Will Smith	Christ. Columbus	Sep 1	Millor Boyd	Keziah Ellen
Jul 14	J. D. Crawford	Amelia Eleanor	14	Milly Blk	Wid. N. adult
24	Will. Poage	Thos Jefferson		Hannah Do	Do N. Do
	John Poage	Rob. Miller	16	Isaac McFaddin	Susan Eliza
Jul 24	Jos Poage	Saml Givens		D. G. Slimon	Joseph John
		Will. Harvey		Tot 3 2d	11 Infants
		Jos. McConnel			

Register Comts from Ap 1834 to Ap 1835

On examination Ap 27 Mary Neely (Wid) Mr McKennon Mrs McKennon, Sidney & Peter (St.) 5

In Certificate Alexander Crawford, Sarah Crawford
Mary Culp 3

Died Florah Currey Isbel Gill. 2

Dismissed I. N. Lewis, Sisley Nelson, Geo Nelson, R.K. Nelson, J. Kennedy, Alexr. Gaston, Mary Gaston Jos. H. Gaston, Mary L. Gaston, Tom Blk, Wm. P. McFadden Mrs McKennon 12

Suspended Mr McKennon 1

Last Report 119 + 5 + 3 − 2 − 12 − 1 = 112 Total

Baptized from Ap. 1834 to Ap 1835

June 22	I. F. Whirry	Harriett Russell	Nov 9	W Boyd of C	Mary Eliza
Jul 29	A Crawford	Mary Jane		M. Farrel	Minerva Jane
Oct 12	John Poage	LeRoy Davies		Total 5	Infants.

Register Comg. for Ap 1835 to Ap 1836.

On examination Ap 4 Sarah L. Poage, ~~Mary~~ ~~Wm. McFadden~~ Aug 1 Jon. N. McElwee, Martha C McElwee, Dav. N Harden Chs Le R Boyd, Sarah R. Boyd, Oct 18 Ann T. Adams, A Crawford Jonathan (Ch; Cynthia Ken, Willey Ken. Harry (Cr, Betsey Mf. Blk. 13

On certificate I. W. Adams Louisa Adams Wm. McFadden 3

Died Sarah Johnston, Eliza Boyd, Sarah Boyd 3

Dismissed L. S. & Wilson, John Gibbon, T. B. Porter 3

61

Last Report 112+13+3-3-3-3 = 122. Total

Baptized from Ap 1835 to Ap 1836 — Total 1 Ad. & 5 Infts

			1836		
Aug 1	D. Boyd	Martha Anne	Mar 1[illegible]	Ro[illegible] C L K Boyd	Mat. Barksdale
2	Jonathan Ch	adult	25	Dr Roland	Hann Susan
Oct 19	D. N. Harden	Eliza Jane Cow[illegible]			Thomas

Register Comm. from Ap 1835 to Ap 1837

August 1st 1835 the following persons were set apart to the office of elder in this church viz

James E McFadden reinstated

Alexander Crawford installed and

William Cowan ordained

Register Comt from Ap 1837 to Ap 1837

On examination Aug 13 Dr. Roland, Margt. E Boyd

Cole, Jenah — Patsy & Betsey 6

Decd. Jane McClure, E C. Gill, Sus. E. Boyd, S. Mahood 4

Dismissed. C L K Boyd S. R Boyd, W P. McFadden, A H

McFadden, Mary B Stuart, Mary Lewis, J. N McElwee

M A. McElwee, Blks Amy & Mary 10

Last Report 122+6-4-10 = 114 Total

Baptized May 2 J P. Dunlap, Isaac LeRoy — J Poage, Mary Jane

May 22 - Jenah Blk — July 3. W P. McFadden Mary Amelia Jane

July 3 J. W. Adams — Jno Davies — Aug 12 Jos Poage — John Jas. Harrison

Aug 13. Cale a Blk — adult — Total 2 Adts & 5 Infants

Hopewell. Ap. 6. 1838 — Approved by Presby — J B Davies Mod —

Register Comts from Ap 1837 to Ap 1838

On examination Jun 17. Chs. B. Kitchen. Oct 1st Mar-

tha E. Boyd, Jane Cowan; James Adams 4

Died, Mary Culp, Milly, Will. Boyd Jan. 18. 1838 3

Dismissed J. H Poage, J C C Gibbes, W Stringfellow

Pat. Stringfellow, R. H. Stringfellow 5

Last Report — 114 + 4 — 3 — 5 = 110 Total

1838 Baptized

Ap 15	W. Boyd	Wm Charles	Sep 10	Jno Poage	Anne Frances
30	J D Crawford	Agnes Isabella		Jonathan	Caroline Amelia
			23	Ellen Boyd	Jane Isabella
May 14	Will Neely	Margt. Anne		Martha Gill	Rob Shelby
Jun 17	D N. Harden	John Harvey			Geo Ripley
Jul 2	Dav Boyd	Agnes Eliza			Ezek. Hale
16	G. H Neely	Will. Chambers			Ths. S. Mills
	Mrs Chambers	Jno Ashcraft			Jno Jas Lauren
Aug 10	A Crawford	Sus. Isabella	Nov 26	J. W Adams	Will. Cooper
Sep 10	Jsa. McFadden	Jas Randolph		Total 20 Infants	
		Josiah Moore			

Nov. 3. 1838

Ordained as Elders in this Church Messrs

John Poage and Geo. H. Neely

Register Communicants from Ap 1838 to Ap 1839

On Examination Ap 29 Martha Gill, Mary Miller
Augt 20 Wilmot S. Gibbes, Vicy E. Neely - Nov 3 Jos S. Poage
Minerva E. Boyd Mary Crawford, Selena Davidson
Isabel Davidson Peter (Miller) Cressy (Gill) Sarah Boyd
& Elizabeth Walls 13
On certificate Louisa Poage - 1

Died. Mary Steele, Jane McClure, Ag. Crawford, Mary
Porter, Mary K. Hardeman 5

Dismissed. Mrs Lowrey, Vicy E Neely, Phillis, Geo. H Miller
and Mary Miller 5
Suspended, David, also Patsy, since dead 2

1839. Baptized } Last report 110 + 13 + 1 − 5 − 5 − 2 = 112.

Apr 28	Rev S.B.O. Wilson	Mary Eliza	Nov. 8	Mary Crawford an Adult	
Jun 21	A. M. Boyd	Francis Marion	1839		
Aug 5	David Boyd	David Lee			
18	Cressy, B.H.	an adult.	Mar 25	Rev. C.L.K Boyd	Susan Jane
Oct 14	Jos. Poage	Alonza Walker			
	J. T. Whiny	Saml. Jonathan	Total	2 adults &	7 Infants
	Jos. S. Poage	Mary Harriett			

1839. Register of Communicants from April 1839 to Apr. 1840
Received August 3. on examination, Margt A. Kelsey
Jonas Rader, Sarah M. Rader, Jas Hickler, Reb. N. Hickler
Tony & Eliza (McFadden) on Sept 1st. Jno Dunlap Eliz. Dunlap

on 15th Sept. Jane C. Neely - on 25th Sept Wid. S. Boyd Eleanor Morris - on Nov. 3rd Jas. H. Crawford, R. A. F. Crawford, Minerva Steele, Thomas L. Neely, Jinsey Adams Moses (Crawford) Mary (Beckham) 19

Received on Certificate, George Agnew, Jane Agnew 2

Died August 16th Rosannah Steele 1

Dismissed Sarah L. Lewis, Eliza Wallis, Dr. C. Boyd & Eliz Boyd 8
Dr. C. B. Hicklin, W. W. Adams

Last Report 112+19+2−1−6= 126

Baptized

Apr	28	J.W. Adams	Calvin	Sept	25	Will. Boyd	David Samuel
Jun	9	D.C. Crawford	Rebec. Robinson			Wid S. Boyd	Mary Eleanor
Aug.	2	Will. Neely	Jas. Hall Gaston				Margt Elizabeth
	3	Geo. Agnew	Katharine Jane				Martha Emeline
	25	A. M. Boyd	Martha Anne				Rob. Geo. Gile
		Mal. Ferrel	Angie Francis			Eleanor Morris	an Adult
		Jonas Rader	Will Pinckney	Nov	4	Mary (Beckham)	Blk adult
			Julius Alexander		+	Tony (McFad)	Blk Adult
	26	All. Gibbes	W. H. Dessausure			and Child	Mary Jane
Sept	1	John Dunlap	Mary Pagan				Geo. Darcy
			Cath. Jones	1840			Alexander
			Anne	Jan	12	Isaac McFadden	Ralph Buford
			Sarah Elizab.	Mar	29	David Boyd	Will. Harris
						Total - 3 Adts	23 Infants

Approved to this page by Bethel Presbytery.
April 3 1841. P.E. Bishop. Moderator.

1840. Register of Communicants from April 1840 to April 1841 - viz Received April 18th Mary Chambers, Jane Gibbey Nancy, Indian - Nov. 1. Margaret Jordon on examination. 4

Died July 28 William Boyd, Jan 29. 1841 Mary Miller Mar 7th Margaret Cowan 3

Dismissed. Mary Poage, Anne Wherry, Martha Gill Rachel Downing, Clem. Downing, Isabel D. Nisbet, Wm Adams Martha Adams, Margaret T. Adams, James Adams, Anne Y. Adams, Jenny Adams, J W. Adams, Louisa Adams, Geo. Agnew, Jane Agnew 16

Last Report 126 + 4 — 3 — 16 = 111

Baptized

Apr 18th John Dunlap John James

Jun 7th Nancy, Indian adult

Jun 7th Jonathan Blk, Jane

28th Dr H D. Gibbes Edward Crawford

July 19th John Poage David Randolph

24 John S. Chambers Stewart Starr

Oct 30 Mr H. Crawford John Alexander. Total 1 Adult & 6 Infants

1841. Register of Communicants from April 1841 to April 1842 &c.

August 15. Received on examination Hugh M. Poage
Margaret Gosby

October 23. Do Do Robert G. Mills

Died Augt 24-1841 Mrs Prudence Selena Mills

Do Oct. 22-1841 Mrs Jane Crawford

Under Suspension. Peter, of Mr Miller, Bessy, of Mr Gill.

Last Report Members 111 added 3, died 2 Susp. 2 Total 110

Baptized May 2. 1841 Anderson M Boyd. Sarah Ellen

Augt 16. Isaac McFadden. Amelia Josephine

Wm P. McFadden Susan Emeline

25. Alester Gibbes Hugh Richardson

September 8 Alex. Pagan Mary Jane

Susanna Eleanor

Sarah Agness

Rob. G. Mills Edwin

Thomas Sumpter

Robert Alexander

Eugenius

Julius

October 23. Jonas Rader Eli Cincinnatus

1841	October 23	James Decker	William Cloud
	December 12[t]	Geo. H. Neely	Selena Mills
		Marg[t]. Jordan	Rob[t]. Henry Hayne
			John Hall
			George Washington

Total baptized 18..

Approved to page 67

April 7th 1842. Wm B. Davies Mod

Remarks

At a called meeting of the Presbytery of Bethel at this church on the day of 1841 the Pastoral relation existing between Rev John B. Davies which had existed for 42 years was dissolved. Faithful as were his services. and long as they were continued, the results must be most important. Many, no doubt at the day of Judgment will rise & call him blessed and who shall be as stars in his crown of rejoicing for ever. But awful must be the guilt & condemnation of such as come short of a saving interest in Christ. It shall then be more tolerable for Sodom & Gomorrah than for them.

1842. Register of communicants from April 1842 until April 1843.

Received on certificate

April 17th 1842 Mrs Rebecca B. Gilland

Jany 15th 1843 Mrs S. A Kelsey

Received on examination

April 16th 1842. Prudence P. Neely

Esther A. Neely

July 30th David D. Neely

Peter, of J. D. Crawford

Eliza of do

Sept 23d. Mack of do

James A. Downey 7,

Died Feby 8th 1842 Robt. G. Mills 1

Dismissed March 13th 1842 Isaac McFadden

Pr last report members 110 added 9 dismissed 1. Died 1=117

Baptized Adults. July 30th 1842 Peter, of Edwd Crawford

Eliza, of J. D. Crawford

Sept 23d 1842. Mack, of do

Infants, April 16th 1842 of David Boyd, Robt Stanhope

June 5th " David Crawford, Edwd Dunlap

July 30th " Henry Crawford. James Pagan

July 30th. 1842 Eliza (Crawford's) Children. Alexander
" James Henry
" Taylor
" Haywood

Oct. 23rd 1842 John Poage. Caroline Eliza
Nov 6th " James & Minerva Poage, Joseph Steele
Nov. 13th. " Henry D. Gibbs & Jane, Wilmot Stewart
Jany 15th. 1843. Wm. & S.A. Kelsey. Frances Catharine
Feby 19th " John S. Chambers, Robert Robison.

Total, Adults 3. Infants 12 = 15

Approved by Presbytery to page
69. A H Caldwell Moderator.
Apr 7. 1843

1843-4

Register of communicants from April 1843
until April 1844.

Received on certificate

July 30th. Robert Stringfellow
" Maria Stringfellow
" Jane Gray.
August 12th. Narcissa Lewis
December 10th Wm Stringfellow & Patience Stringfellow
6

1843-4

Received on examination

May 20th. James H Wherry
" Ferreby Gill
" Mary Caroline Gibbes
" Hannah (Alex Crawford)
August 19th. Jane Kelsey
" David H. Miller
" Maria (Mrs Lewis) 7.

Dismissed. Robt. L. R. Miller. May 20. 1

May 20. Restored Peter (Mr Miller) 1

Died. Sept 13. Louisa Pray
Nov 2nd Rebecca B. Gillands
Nov - Mrs David Boyd
Nov 5. Mary R. Crawford
Nov 17. Mary J. Wherry
Dec 23. Patience Stringfellow
March 7. Molly Neely. 7.

Baptized. Adults.
May 20th Ferreby Gill
" Hannah (Alex Crawford) 2

Infants.
May 20th. Hannah Crawfords Children

Nanny & Scylla
Feby 18. Jonathan (cherry's) Hannah.
March 10. Robert Stringfellow, Edwin Hall, John James, Patience Amelia, & William J.

Last report 117+6+7+1-1-7 = Total 123.

Resolutions of Session March 31st 1844.

Whereas, The General Assembly of the Presbyterian church, did, during its sessions in 1843. decide, that any three ministers of a Presbytery, being regularly convened are a quorum, competent to the transaction of all business. (See minutes, page 196) Therefore.

Resolved. 1. That Presbyterianism is republican in its nature, requiring a representation in all its assemblies, both of the ministry and laity, and consequently contemplating the presence of the Eldership as essential to constitute a quorum for the transaction of Presbyterial business.

Resolved 2. That the decision of the last General assembly on this subject, derogates from the importance, and subverts the rights of the Eldership, and is contrary to the genius of the Republicanism of Presbytery.

72 Resolved 3. That said decision of the General assembly ought to be reversed, and the true position given to the Eldership, which they ought to occupy in our Ecclesiastical Assemblies.

Resolved 4. That there is no quorum, and that Presbytery cannot be constituted, without the presence of Ruling Elders.

Resolved 5. That we, as the session of Fishing Creek church, will not give our sanction or support to any delegate to the assembly of 1844. whose sentiments are not avowedly in accordance with the spirit of these resolutions, and who will not pledge himself to use his efforts to procure a decision in that assembly, giving to the Eldership their true position in Presbytery. J. R. Gilland. Moderator

N. B. These records, thus far, were approved by the Presbytery of Bethel, during its sessions at Catholic church. April 1844. but neglected to be attested by the moderator.

1844. Register of communicants from April 1844 until April 1845.

Received on certificate

April 27th 1844 Dr Wm H. Stringfellow

Sept 8th " Mrs Mary Robison 2

Restored Sept 27th - Samuel Boyd 1

Received on examination

April 27th. Mary Jane Crawford

" Agnes Jane Neely

" James E. Boyd

Sept. 7th. Mary Narcissa Neely

" James (of Edward Crawford)

" Wilson (of Wm Poag)

8th - John Newton Neely

Oct 3rd John Leander Boyd

" Rachel Clarentine Boyd

Nov 10th. Wm Henry Chambers 10

<u>Died</u>

June 10th David Boyd

Sept 26th Charles Boyd (Ruling Elder) Jefferson,

Nov 14th. James E. McFadden Ruling Elder

Dec 6th - Mrs Agnes Porter

74 1845 Jany 19th Jos. Steele Pogy 5

Infants Baptized.

Sept 1st. of Jas Henry Crawford. Sarah La Fayette
Oct 3rd " Saml. Boyd. Wm. Lawrence
" " " David Caldwell
" " " Margaret Isabella
" " " Thomas Henry
Nov 10th. Wm. H. Chambers, Sarah Jane
" " " " John Kelsey
" " " " Agnes Lucretia.
Nov 17th. James Hicklin. Jane Victoria.
Dec 29th Dr. H. D. Gibbes, Henry Desaussure 10

Adults Baptized.

Sept 7th James. servant of Edward Crawford
" Wilson " of Wm. Pogy
Oct 3rd. John Leander Boyd
" Rachel Clorentine Boyd.
Nov 10th. William Henry Chambers 5
Total Baptized 15

Dismissed

June 2nd D. N. Hardin
Dec 1st William Cowan
" Jane Cowan 3

By last report 123+24+10-5-3 = Total 127

Approved by Presbytery at Ebenezer
April 9. 1845   J L Watson Mod Pres

1845–6.

Register of communicants from April 1845 to April 1846.

Received on examination

April 26th 1845. Mary Jane Poag. Luvicy S. Poag. Cynthia McCullough. Jane S. Neely. Elias a servant of Wm Poag. Riley of do. Frank of do. John of do.   8

August 18. James W. Miller   1

Sept 20 & 21. Rachel A Boyd. James M. Poag. William Poag. John Leroy Neely. Margaret Jane Stringfellow. Robert Jennings Boyd.   6

Servants. Charles and Harry (of Wm Poag) Randolph (McFadden) Wiley (Gill), Peter (Miller) Milley & Betsey of do. Paris (Gibbes) Aggy (Gill), Lilly (McFadden) Aindy (Kelsey) Cynthia (Chambers) Esther (do; Drumalda (do. Paulina (J. Poag) Betsey (Crawford) Aggy (Neely) Rainey (Crawford)   18

Total   33

Restored at same time Gracey (Gill) 1.

Dismissed May 18. John N. Neely. Sep 20. James E. Boyd Oct 10. Robt Jennings Boyd. Dec 28 Keziah Boyd & Margaret Boyd. 5

Departed this life April 28. Edward Crawford (Elder) June 7. Eliza J. Neely. Dec 20. Mary Robison Jany 19. /46 Thomas E. Neely. 4

Infants Baptized.

April 25. Of Jonas Rader, Sarah Jane.
May 18. James & M. Pogg Rosanna Jane
July 10 Cynthia McCullough Saml. Leonard
" " Mary Rosanna
" " Margaret Auban
" " Wm Taylor
" " John Lawrence
Sep 20. Tomely Gill, Arch. La Fayette.

Sep 20 Isaac McFadden Rufus Durelle.
John Pogg George Theodore
Tony's (C. McFadden) Children
" Agnes Lucinda
" Georgianna
Rainey (Crawford's) children
Narcissa & Ben

Total 14.

Adults Baptized April 26. Elias (Wm Pogg) Riley do Frank do. John do.

Sep. 20 & 21. Charles & Harry (Wm Pogg) Randolph (McFadden) Wiley (Gill) Peter (Miller) Milley (do) Betsey (do) Paris (Gill) Aggy (Gill) Lilley (McFadden) Andy (Kelley) Cynthia (Chambers)

Esther. do. Irumalda. do. Paulina (Boyd) Betsey (Crawford)
Affy (Neely) Rainey (Crawford) 22.

Elders Elected April 26. John S. Chambers. Robert Stringfellow. J. Harvey Crawford & Joseph Steele. all of whom were ordained and installed except the last, who was absent & unwell & who afterwards declined...

By last report. 127 + 8 + 1 + 6 + 33 + 1 − 5 − 4 = 168

Approved by Presbytery thus far.
A. H. Caldwell

1846–7.

Register of communicants from April 1846 to April 1847.

Received on examination

May 9th 1847. Joseph W. Steele. Lilly (Crawford) Lydia
Chambers. Martha (Boyd) Isaac (Crawford)
October 10th. Charlotte (Miller). Delila (McCullough)
" 11th Lavina E. Steele. 8

Died during the year.

Jany 22nd 1847. William Poag. Senr. Feby 4. Elias (Poag)
Feby 17. Minerva S. Poag 3

Dismissed. April 5th David Dunlap Neely 1

Infants Baptized.

May 9th 1846. of Mrs Jane Neely. Louisa Irene Thomas.

" " John S. Chambers. William.

" " James R. Gilland. James Rust.

" " J. Henry Crawford. Mary Gill.

May 10th. of Isaac (Crawford) James Henry.

" " Lilly (Crawford) Adeline & Susan.

" " Lilly (McFadden) Charlotte Caroline Thomas Henry, and Alexander

July 13th. of Jonathan (Cherry) Amelia.

Oct. 11. Peter (Crawford) Levi and Eliza

" Paulina (Poag) Eliza & James Alexander.

" Isaac (Crawford) Mary Rebecca.

Jany 17. 1847 of G. H. Neely. Margaret Eugenia. 17

Adults Baptized.

May 10. 1846. Lilly (Crawford) Lydia (Chambers) Martha (Saml. Boyd) Isaac (Crawford)

Oct 11. Charlotte (Miller) Delila (McCullough). 6.

By last report 168 + 8 - 3 - 1 = 172.

Approved by Bethel Presbytery at its sessions at Upper Catholic. April 1847 W. R. Gilland. Moderator.

1847–8.

Register of communicants from April 1847 to April 1848.

Received on examination,

September 25th 1847. George (Chambers) & Harriet (Millar) 2

Died during the year,

Sept 24th 1847 Mrs Jane Boyd. widow of Wm Boyd 1

March 29th 1848 George (Chambers) 2

Dismissed, April 2nd 1848 Mrs Margaret Heffley 1

Infants Baptized.

April 18th 1847. Child of James M. Bag, named Wm Minerva Joan

" " of Aggy (Gill) — — Adam

May 13th — of Isaac McFadden — Alice

" " of Wm H. Chambers — Sarah Agnes

" 15th of Charlotte (Miller) Melinda Jane

Sep 24th. of James R & M. C. Gillard — Wilmot Francis

Nov 14th of Gracey (Gill) — Susan Caroline, Saml. Henry,

" Mary Emeline, George, Aaron,

" James Flanagan, Joanna

Jany 16th 1848. of David C & Mary Crawford. — Martha Jane

April 2nd - of J. H and Rebecca Crawford. — Robert Mills 15.

Adults Baptized. Sep 24th George (Chambers. Harriet (Millar) 2

Received on Certificate

May 13th 1847 Isaac McFadden certificate returned

April 2nd 1848 William Henry Steele and Mary Steele 3

Thus the record would stand 172+2-2-1+3 = 174.

But in carefully examining the list of communicants there can only be found 98 whites and 51 blacks, total 149

Approved April 6th 1848

Wm B Davies Mod

1848.

Register from April 1848 until November 1848.

Died during that period.

April 16. Mrs Mary McFadden

Sept. 20 Rainey Crawford.

Dismissed Sept 25. Wm Henry Steele & Mrs Mary Steele.

Infants baptized.

June 18. Of Riley (Bag) James Munroe.

" Andy (Kelsey) Frank Nancy & Mary Ann. &

" " " George & Caroline

" Jonathan (Cherry) Thomas Henry.

Wm H. Steele. Wm Samuel & Rufus Aurelius.

Aug 4. Rev J. R & M. C. Gilland, Thomas McDowell.

Sept 23. Of P. H & Margt Neely. John Harvey
" J. S & Mary Chambers Mary Lucretia.
" Wm H Chambers — David Jackson.

Gave for Educational purposes April 30. $15.00
" For Foreign Missions Sept 23. 36.75
" For Publication & Colportage April 30. 10.00

On the First of November, the ministerial services of Rev James R. Gillan ceased with this congregation. The results of his labours for seven years, wanting two months will not be known until the day of Eternity. May Pastor & people have a joyful meeting in the kingdom of Heaven.

79 Added during ministry of J.R.G.
42 Whites. 37 Blacks : 30 Whites on Examination, 12 whites by Certificate.

1848. Nov. 1st. Ministerial services of Rev. Arnold Wm Miller commenced as Supply of Fishing Creek Church.

1849.

Marriages.

April 18th Mrs Margaret Boyd to John F. Workman
May 30th Wm Porter & Martha E. Boyd
July 26th Isaac McFadden & Mrs Jane Neely 3

Infant Baptized.

April 21st of Jas W. Miller, Esther Jane, born 22d Oct. 1848.

Received on Certificate

April 21st, 1849. Mrs. Sarah B. Miller 1

Restored, April 21st, Lilly (Crawford).

Departed this life,

Jan. 10th, 1849. Wm. H. Chambers

May 22d " Wm. Stringfellow (formerly, Elder)

June 16th " Betsey (McFadden) ,3

Received on examination

Oct. 20th, 1849. Martha Neely, Samuel Woodburn

October 20th 1849. Rev. Arnold W. Miller ordained & installed Pastor of Fishing Creek Church.

Received on examination,

October 28th Wm. Duncan.

Dismissed, Nov. 5th, Dr. Wm. Rowland & Mrs. Susan P. Rowland

Infants baptized.

Nov. 9th of Robt. A. Stringfellow, Lucius Gray, born 15th August 1848

" of Wm. Duncan, Lurenna Urissa, born 22d April 1849

Received on examination, Nov. 10th, Margaret Lewis.

Died, Dec. 17th Mary (Boyd)

4th Sabbaths in April and September were fixed upon by Session for stated Communion Seasons.

1849. Testimony against Dancing.

Two instances occurring of indulgence in this Sin — one under very aggravating circumstances; taking place the night before the preparatory services of the Communion — by many of the Youth of the Church: the following Paper was adopted by the Session June, 1849. and ordered to be read in the presence of the Congregation.

The Session of this Church have marked with painful anxiety the prevalence of worldly amusements in the community. They have noticed with deep concern a disposition on the part of some members of the Church to permit their children to engage in dancing. The Session regard this amusement, with others of a similar character, as sinful, offensive in the sight of God, as exerting a most pernicious influence on the minds & morals of the Young;

tending to produce a levity of character, to banish serious impressions from their minds, generate a settled indifference to the claims of religion, harden their hearts and prove fatal to the interests of their immortal souls. Ungodly Amusements are the Sacraments of the World, instituted by him, whom the Scriptures term the 'God of this World'. And as at the Sacraments of the Church, Christians renew their allegiance to their Lord, Jesus Christ, so also, in assemblies for worldly amusements, worldly persons at these their Sacraments, consecrate themselves soul & body, afresh, to Satan, their Lord & Master. They but obey his behest, whilst they imagine they are serving only their own pleasure.

So far from being "innocent amusements" they are public, testimonials of devotion to his service.

If it be wrong for Christians to en=

gage in the dance, it is wrong for all others to do the same. For precisely the same obligations rest upon the world as upon Christians. And if it be sinful for Christian parents to indulge in this amusement, it is equally sinful in them to suffer their children to do the same. For God holds them responsible for all sinful acts which they allow in the children subject to their control. It is mentioned in Scripture to the reproach of Eli, that his sons acted wickedly and he restrained them not God declares that He judged Eli for the iniquity of his sons. It is also laid down in God's Word as a distinguishing mark of the ungodly that they encouraged or allowed <u>dancing</u> in their families. In Job (21 : 11) we read – "They send forth their little ones like a flock and <u>their children dance</u>". It is next added - "Therefore they say unto God, Depart from us, for we desire not the knowledge of Thy ways. What is the Almighty that we should serve Him?" - If then this practice be countenanced in our midst by Christian Parents, we may expect the Judgment of God to rest upon our Church. God will withdraw His Spirit from us, send leanness into our souls, make His own ordinances barren, so that they shall cease to be a medium through which we receive spiritual strength, comfort & Joy. 'Ichabod' will then be written upon our Temple - our glory will have departed.

The Session, responsible to God for the purity of this Church, over whom the Holy Ghost hath made them overseers, do hereby call upon the members to discountenance and forbid their children engaging in these amusements of an ungodly world, and do now solemnly admonish them that a failure to exercise for the future, their just & lawful authority over their children, will subject them to the discipline of the Church. And they would also remind the children of the Church that though not in communion with us, which it is their bounden duty to be, yet they are, equally with Professors, members of this Church & subject to its government & discipline — according to the teachings of Scripture and of our Book of Discipline which, in Section 5th, Chap. 1st, thus declares, "All baptized persons are members of the Church, are under its care, and subject to its government and discipline: and when they have arrived at the years of discretion, they are bound to perform all the duties of church members"

"—The Session solemnly call upon such of them as were recently engaged in the worldly amusement herein specified and condemned, to repent of their sin before God, and they admonish them against the future commission of this offence, which will expose them to the censures of the Church. They entreat them not to treat with indifference, or despise the ordinance of God, lest they bring swift destruction on their own souls.

Examined and approved in Presbytery
Apl. 4th 1850
D. I. Auld
Mod

1850–1

Register from April 1850 to April 1851.

Received on Examination.

April 7th Dr. Jno. T. Goudelock, Margaret J. Crawford
" 26th Edwin Mills.
" 27th Elizabeth Boyd.

1850. 17

April 28th Mrs Margaret Agurs, Greene (Neely)

Sept. 21st Frank (Crawford)

" 22d Mrs Amanda Crawford. Ed. Newton Crawford. 8.

Received on Certificate.

Sept. 21st Robt. Jennings Boyd. Certificate returned.

Adults Baptized.

April 21st Dr Jas. J. Goudelock.

" 28th Greene (Neely)

Sept 22d Frank (Crawford) 3

Infants Baptized.

April 21st of Jas. Wherry, Eliza Jane, born 28th August 1849.

" 28th of Edwin Mills, Selina Eugenius, born 23 Dec. 1848.

" " of Mrs Isabella Boyd, Lorenzo Verennes, born

" 28th of Riley (Prag) Thos Leonard, of Paulina (Prag) Isaac Sylvanus.

May 19th of David C. Crawford, Mary Hope, born Feb. 10th, 1850.

" " of J. Harvey Crawford, Geo. Harvey. born April 12th 1850.

June 9th of Jonathan (Cherry) Margaret Paulina

Sept. 21st of Jennings Boyd, Jas Caldwell, born 11th Aug. 1849.

" 20th of Wm Duncan, Rosaline Isabella, born July 11th 1850. 10.

Restored

April 28th Aggy (Cathcart) Sept 21st Wm Neely.

Dismissed

July 28th Jas. Hicklin & Rebecca Hicklin

1850

August 16th Mrs Caroline Gilland 3.

Married.

May 9th Dr Jas. T. Goudelock & Agnes Jane Neely.

July 23rd Rev. A. W. Miller & Margaret Jane Stringfellow

Feb. 13th 1851. Jas. M. Poag & Broach

Died.

Jan. 5th 1851. Robt. Jennings Boyd.

Feb. 2d 1851. Alexander Crauford (Elder)

Gave,

April 28th 1850.	For Foreign Missions	$30,00
Sept 22d "	For Domestic Missions	42,00
March 16th 1851.	For Assem. Commiss. & Education Fund	~~[illegible]~~ 26,00

Examined & Approved in Presbytery

April 3rd 1851. A. W. Miller, Moderator

1851-2

Register from April 1851 to April 1852.

Received on Examination.

April 26th, Mrs Mary Blake.

September 28th, Mrs Julia Farley, Frances Agurs, Sarah Neely.

September 29th, Mrs Martha McElwee, Emily McElwee, Sally Wherry,
" Harriet Wherry, Susan Crawford, Agnes Crawford.
1852, Jan. 4th, Mary Jane Steele, Elizabeth Workman, Peter (McCullough) 13.

Adults Baptised.

1851. Sept. 27th. Mrs Julia Harley, Frances Agnes.
1852. Jany. 4th, Mary Jane Steele, Peter (McCullough) 4.

Infants Baptised.

1851. April 25th, of Jno. S. Chambers, Margaret Annette, born March 5th 1851.
" " of Dr Goudelock, Mary Selina, born Feb. 13th 1851.
" " of Edwin Mills, Mary Amelia, born Dec. 28th 1850.
" April 26th, of Jas. W. Miller, Robt. Davies, born
" July 5th of Mrs Margaret Workman, Margaret Deborah, born Dec. 21st 1850.
" August 17th Robert Eveline Harrison Hartness, Grandson of
Mr Jas. Gill, aged 10 yrs, parents both dead, bapt. on faith of Mr Gill, as sponsor
" September 26th of Wm Robinson, Jas. Marion, born March 18th 1851.
1852. Jany. 3rd, of Rev. A W & Mrs J. Miller, Augustine, born June 11th 1851.
" " 25th of Robt. Stringfellow, Maria Catharine, born May 13th 1850.
" " " of Isaac McFadden, William Stanley, born
10.

Dismissed.

1851. April 25th Mrs Isabella Boyd, Rachel Boyd.
" May 25th Mrs Lavina Pressley. Dec. 14th Martha (Boyd)
1852 Jany 4th Wm Duncan & Minerva Duncan. 6.

 Suspended:

1851. August 17th Harry (Craufurd).

" Resolution! June 1st Session fixed upon First Sabbath in Jany, April, July & Last in Sept. as regular Quarterly Comm. Seasons of F. C. Church.

" Election. July 5th James Wherry & Edwin Mills, elected Elders.

" August 17th, Jas. Wherry & Edwin Mills (Ruling Elders Elect) Ordained & Installed.

Married.

1851. June 12th, Margaret I. Craufurd to Mr. Wilfong.

" August 6th, Jane C. Neely to Mr. Jno. Goudelock.

1852 Mary Jane Pray to Dr. Stewart.

" February 19th Frances Agurs to Mr. Turner Morgan. 4

Died.

1852. Feby 11th Wm. Neely.

" March 9th Mrs. Mary Pagan.

Gave

1851	April 27th.	For Foreign Missions	$47,25
"	Sept. 29th.	For Domestic Missions.	36,55
1852	Jany 4th.	For Education	20,00
"	March 21st.	For Assembly's Commiss. & Conting. Fund.	18,66¼
			$122,46¼

1851. Tuesday, August 12th Rumour having

charged several of the colored members of this church with expressing sentiments hostile to the institution of Slavery – denying the lawfulness of the relation & affirming the right of the slave to the proceeds of his his own labour – a meeting was held by Session this day (Tuesday) for the purpose of investigating the charges. About half a dozen servants appeared; some together with their masters. Upon making the object of their summons known & after interrogating them, it appeared that some were falsely charged; others admitted frankly that they had given utterance to improper expressions, of which they repented; and others again (whose sincerity was doubted) denied all knowledge of the entire matter. They were instructed again out of the Scriptures respecting their duty, faithfully admonished against the cultivation of a rebellious spirit, exhorted to obedience & fidelity to the interests of their earthly masters, as one test of their obedience to the Lord Jesus Christ, Who Himself had appointed their lot; and were commended to a constant study to adorn the doctrine of God their Saviour in all things. They then express. themselves satisfied, and were dismissed after prayer. — This meeting, we trust, will have a salutary influence upon our colored community for a long time to come. — — — — —

1852. March 21st Session being convened, Mr. Jno. Chambers & Mr. Robt. Stringfellow (Elders) communicated to Session that during their late absence from the State, they had travelled, the first-named, thrice, the second, twice, upon the Sabbath day & mentioned the circumstances in which they were placed. Mr. Chambers stated, that in the first instance, he had, whilst travelling in ArKansas, put up on Saturday evening at a Tavern, where it was his intention to have remained quietly through the Sabb. but, on the next morning, such was the noise and disorder of the crowd that collected there, preventing him from a proper observance of the day, that he thought it best to leave the place and go into the country, to the house of a relative, some miles distant. This he did, hiring no conveyance whatever, but walking. His sole motive was to escape the company at the Tavern & spend the Sabbath in a more proper way than he could have done otherwise.

The Second instance, which occurred some time after; he had been travelling upon a steamboat previous to the Sabbath & during that day, left the boat, for another - both boats continuing their trips.

The Third instance; he had been travelling in a stage for some time & being in ill health, became quite sick & weak & felt compelled to leave the stage for a more suitable mode of conveyance. The only opportunity that occurred or was likely to occur for some time, was presented in a Steamboat, leaving the place where he arrived the evening before, on

Sabbath morning. He entered the boat & spent the day in his room, in the private reading of the Bible. The stage would not have stopped upon the Sabbath & he would probably have reached the place of his destination sooner by it, than by the boat.

Mr Stringfellow stated that whilst in Florida, he & his party had lodged one Saturday evening in a very open, ~~exposed~~ building & the next morning, they left it for a comfortable lodging a few miles distant, where they remained all day.

Second instance. They had put up on Saturday evening at a Tavern, where they expected to remain the Sabbath day. The next morning having left the Tavern for a little while; he found, on his return, that one of the party had, unexpectedly to him, hired a conveyance and was preparing to start. Against his wish, he was in a measure compelled to travel, for they had previously to this, sold their horses & were without a conveyance

His remonstrances produced no effect. — — — The Session, having heard these statements, sustained the excuses of these brethren. — —
A call for any other cases of similar nature that had come to the knowledge of any member, being made it was then stated (what, in fact Rumour had charged previously) that Mr Isaac McFadden had travelled in the cars from Charleston to Columbia on the Sabbath day. It was also stated that he had, when in Florida, hired a conveyance on Sabbath morning and travelled on that day. – It being ascertained that Mr McFadden was on the ground whilst this meeting was held, Session sent out a member to him, requesting him to appear & give reasons for his conduct. This he refused to do. Session then resolved to let the matter lie over until next Sabbath, as all of the members were not present at this meeting. ——
1852. March 28th, Session met by previous appointment. It was resolved to appoint

a Committee to converse with Mr. McFadden and in a kind and Christian spirit exhort him to appear before Session, representing to him that a refusal to comply was disobedience to the constituted authority of the Church. — Messrs. Jno. Boag & Jno. Chambers were appointed the Committee — — — — —

All meetings of Session were opened & closed with Prayer

Examined & approved to this page.
J. M. H. Adams Modr.
of Bethel Presbytery.

1852 – 3.

Register from April 1852 to April 1853.

Received on Examination.

April 9th. Mary J. Pagan, Mrs. Nancy Boag.
" 10th Rebecca Workman, Mrs. Amelia McFadden
" " Melinda McFadden, Susan McFadden
" " Ann (Neely).
July 4th John Malony.
Sept. 25th: Mrs. Margt. Steele, Mary Jane Boag,

Received on exam.

Sept. 25th. Martha Poag, Sarah Pagan "

" " Amos (McFadden) Benjamin (Poag)

" " Maria (Rader), Jane (Downey), Mary (Neely)

" " Amanda (Poag); Lila (Poag), William (Crawford),

" " Allen (chambers)

" 26th Mrs E. N. Crawford.

Jany 8th 1853. Randolph McFadden.

March 13th " G. W. Harris.

Jany 9th " Sena ( ) Adeline (McFadden), Anne (Wilfong) 27.

Received on Certificate

1852. Sept 25 - J. W. Wilfong. 1/28

Adults Baptized.

1852. April 10th Ann (Neely), Sept. 25th Allen (chambers)

" Sept. 25th Maria (Rader), Mary & child (Neely).

" " " " Jane (Downey)

1853. Jany. 9th Amos (McFadden), Ben (Poag), Rebecca (Wilfong). 8

Infants Baptized.

1852. June 6th of J. Harvey Crawford, Julius Green, born

" Sept. 25th of J.W. Wilfong, Sarah Ann Elizabeth, born

" of Jas F. Wherry, James born

" Dec. 12th of Edwin Mills, Helen Agnes born

" Dec. 19th of David Crawford, born

Infants Baptized.

1853. Jany. 23rd of Dr Goudelock, Adam John, born

1852. Sept. 25th of Mary (Neely) 7

Restored.

1852. April 10th. Mrs Kerreby Workman.

" Sept 26th. Joumalda (Chambers), Harry (Crawford) 3

Married.

1852. July 8th. Edward N. Crawford to Miss [illegible] Aske

" August 26th Miss Melinda McFadden to Mr T. S. Fayssoux

1853. Jany. 24th J. Leroy Neely & Martha Neely.

" March 9th Miss Margt. Lewis to Mr R. McCalla. 4.

Died:

1852. Sept. 11th Wilmot S. Gibbes.

" Oct. 29th Jas. Gill

" Sept. 25th Mrs Amanda Crawford

" Dec. 7th Robt. Miller

1853 Jany. 4th Miss Sally Ellen Wherry.

" March 3rd Mrs Frances Morgan.

1852. Sept. Peter (Miller) Betsey (Miller) 8

Gave, 1852, April 11th For Foreign Missions $33,22
" July 4th For Chickasaw Mission (Watson's) 25,00
" Sept. 26th For Domestic Missions 60,65
1853 Jany. 9th For Assem. Com & Edu. Fund 23.00

$141,87

101

1852. April 9th. The Committee appointed to converse with Mr. McFadden, reported that they had performed the duty assigned them. They were unable to say whether he would come before Session or not, as he neither promised nor refused positively. They hoped he would think better of it & comply with our request. Session then resolved to let the matter lie over until next sabbath.

April 18th. Mr. McFadden case resumed.

After an interchange of opinion, it was resolved to postpone action upon this subject until this day 6 weeks with the design of dealing tenderly & in a Christian spirit with Mr. McF. and with the view of giving him further time to reflect upon his conduct & of opening the door for repentance. Should he however still refuse to appear before Session, Session resolved in that case to issue its first formal citation, in accordance with requisition of Book of Discipline. Messrs. Pong & Chambers were re-appointed the Committee, with the addition of Mr Stringfellow, to converse with Mr Mc K. & induce him, if possible, to appear before Session, as is his duty, & not to cast contempt upon the authority of the Church. They were also instructed to notify him of the proceedings in his case.—

June 6th 1852. Mr Mc K's case resumed. Of the Committee appointed to converse with him, Mr Stringfellow alone had discharged that duty. His report was that he did not judge it probable that Mr Mc K. would appear before Session. It was then resolved that the Committee be continued & directed to see & converse with Mr Mc K. before next Sabbath & in case of his not appearing on that day, that then he be formally cited as Book of Dis. directs.

June 13th 1852. Mr Mc K's case resumed. Two of the Committee Messrs Boaz & Chambers reported that they had called on Mr Mc K. but did not see him. Mr Stringfellow

reported that he had conversed with him, & Mr Mc K expressed himself dissatisfied with the visits of the Committee, saying he was quite tired of the business.
The Committee having failed to effect its object, it was then resolved to cite him formally to appear before Session on 27th June. The citation was issued on Wednesday 16th June, & was delivered on the same day by a member of Session. (The facts in the case, viz: travelling in both instances on the Sabbath, were admitted by him to the Committee)
June 27th '52. A letter directed to Mod & Sess. from Mr K. was read which Session would not receive except as intimating a refusal to appear.
It was then stated by a member of Session that he had an interview with Mr Mc K. that day, who then expressed his willingness to appear

before Session on some weekday. In view of this statement, Session desirous of affording every opportunity, resolved to adjourn their meeting until Next Saturday at 8 o'clock A.M.

July 3rd Saturday. Mr Mc H appeared and upon the Mod. stating the charges against him, he then, after conversation admitted the offence, professed regret & would endeavour to avoid offending in like Manner in future. Session considered this statement satisfactory & thus terminated this unpleasant business.

— All Meetings of Session opened & closed with Prayer & in every case, a Majority, and in almost all, the whole Session was present — — — — —

April 1st 1853 approved by Bethel Presbty S L Watson Mod. Presby

Register from April 1853 to April 1854

Received on Examination...

April 9th, Cynthia Aguers, Susan Aguers
April 3rd George (Crawford)
April 8th Angeline (Mc Culloch)
July 2d Lizzie (Chambers), Esther (Mc Fadden)
July 3rd Becky (Crawford), Fred (Simpson)
Sept 23rd Mrs Ralph Mc Fadden, Sarah (Baskins)
Sept. 24th Margt Louisa Poag, Sam (Crawford)
" " Mary (Crawford), Leidy (Porter) Likey (Poag)
" " Daniel (Poag) William (Gondelock), Barnet (Aguers)
18.

Adults Baptized

April 9th Cynthia Aguers, Susan Aguers
April 8th Angeline (Mc Culloch)
July 3rd Lizzie (Chambers) Becky (Crawford)
Sept. 23rd Sarah (Baskins) Sept. 24th Sam (Crawford)
Sept. 24th Mary (Crawford), Leidy (Porter), Likey (Poag),
" " Daniel (Poag) William (Gondelock)
Sept 25th Barnet (Aguers)
13.

226

Infants Baptized

April 8th Harriet Ann, inf. of Wm Robinson, born Dec. 31st '52.
April 9th : Amelia Buford, inf of Rev. A. Miller, born Jany. 29th '53.
July 1st Mary Harper, inf of Mrs Stewart, Saml. Ashe of Ed. N. Crawford
August. of Peter (Crawford), Rachel Rebecca, Frances Delilah, William Narcissa, Peter Simpson, 8

Restored.

Sept 24th Affy (Neely) 1

Suspended.

May 15th Andy (Adams). July 2d Tony (McFadden) 2

Dismissed.

April 9th Paulina Neely. July 2d David Crawford & Mary Crawford
July 2d Mrs McCullough. Sept. 19th Mr & Mrs Wm Poag. 6.

Married.

Oct. 19th. Mary Jane Poag to Dr Melton

Died.

March 30th Isaac (Crawford) Greene (Neely)
June 25th Wm Porter
March 19th 1854. Mrs Margaret I. Miller
March 22d 1854. Mrs Mary Jane Mills. 5.

Gave. April 10th to Foreign Missions $ 75,00
July 3rd to Education 30,00
Sept 25 to Domestic Missions 55,00
Jany. 15th 1854 to Assembly's Commis 10,00
$ 170,00

All meetings of Session opened & closed with prayer, & in all a majority, & almost all, the entire Session present.

Approved by Bethel Presbytery April 1 1854
P. E. Bishop Moderator

1854–1855

Register from April 1854 to April 1855.

Received on Examination

April 7th 1854. Mrs Mary E. Brown
April 8th Aleck (Crawford), Wilson (Poag)
April 9th Mary (Crawford)
July 2d Flora (Poag)
Sept 23rd Miss Martha Boyd. 6.

Received by Certificate.
Dec. 30th Wm & Jane M. Duncan. 2.

Adults Baptised.
April 8th Wilson (Poag)
April 9th Wm & George (Crawford), Mary (Crawford). 4.

Infants Baptised.
April 7th Nora Hall of Jno. S. Chambers

Infants Baptized.

April 30th Peter, Tilda, John, Martha Angelina, of Peter (McCulloch)
June 11th Rebecca Jane, of Mrs Workman, Mary Ellen of Mr Wilfong
June 25th Jas. Edward of George (Crawford)
" " Wm Alexander & of Angelina (McCulloch)
July 1st Mary Elizabeth, Vincent Brown & Margt. Julianna
of Ralph McFadden –
July 1st Thornton of Robt. H. Stringfellow, Rachel Elizbth of Dr Goudelock
Dec. 30th Mary of Mrs Amelia McFadden.
Oct 22d Rebecca Sumpter of Harvey Crawford.
" " James Gaston of Mrs McCalla. 17.

Suspended. May 21st, Jane Kelsey. July 1st Mrs Margt McCall.
Sept. 24th. Barnet (Agurs). July 1st Betsey (Miller) 4.

Dismissed. May 21st Jo. Steele Sr. Sept 23d Mrs M.
E. Workman, Rebecca M. Workman, Elizebth D. Workman
Mrs Jane C. Goudelock. Sept 24th. Ferreby Workman
Dec. 17th Mrs Graham. Sept 22d Harry (Crawford)
July 1st Harry & Amanda (Poag) 10.

Deacons Elected
July 1st
J. L. Neely, Saml. Woodburn, Jas D Crawford, J. H. Miller, J. W. Wilfong. 5
ordained in August.

Married. Nov. 30th 1854. Mr. Peter & ~~[illegible]~~ Charles Boyd. 97 107

Died. Sept. 10th Jane Kelsey [in humble reliance on Christ]
Oct. 9th David H. Miller (Deacon)
Feby. 8th 1855. Isaac McFadden.
Feby 21st 1855. John Kelsey.
Lizzie (Chambers) 5.

Gave
April 9th To Foreign Missions (Waldenses) $ 60,00
Sept 24th To Domestic Missions $ 60,00
Dec. 31st Assem. Commiss. $ 12,00
$ 13 2,00

(50 copies "Home & Foreign Record" subscribed for by the Congregation.

Meetings of Session opened & Closed with Prayer.

Up to this date April 1st 1855, 79 Persons added to H.C. Church during Ministry of A.W. Miller: 45 Whites, 34 Blacks. 77 on Examina. 2 on Certif.

Examined & approved
Saml G. White (Mod)

Register from April 1853 to 1856.

Recd on Examination

April 28th Miss Anna Francis Poag
Sept 30th Mrs Amanda Reid
Oct 7th Mrs Mary Drennan*
" Miss Mary A Drennan
" " Maria L A Drennan
" " Martha A Drennan
Oct 12th Mrs Nancy Drennan 7
" 13th Anne (Drennan) & Susan (J D Crawford)
" March 29th Hanna (Mrs Mary Drennan) Malinda (R A Crawford)
" 30th George (Downing) 5

Recd by Certificate Frank (Wm Rosborough) 1

Adults Baptized

Oct 7th Misses Mary A. M. L. A & Martha A Drennan.
March 30th Hanna (Drennan) Malinda (Crawford)
George (Downing) 6.

Infants Baptized

April 28th Laura Ellen of Ralph McFadden

Jane Elleanor " Wm Dunkin

A Wm Boyer " Jas F. Wherry

May 26th Edward Alexander " E N Crawford

Sept 30th. Susan " J L Neely

March 29th (1856) Henry Colman " Mrs Mary E Brown 6

" 30th. girl (child) " Jinny (Downing) 1/7

Suspended March 29th Mary (J D Crawford)

March 30th (Peter (McCollough) 2

Dismissed, April 29th Mrs M. J. Stewart.

Mrs M McCollough Jas Downing. 3

Restored to Communion,

April 28th Mrs M McCollough

Oct. 14th Andy (Miller) Adaline (Jas McFadden)

Aggy (G H Neely) Tony (Ralph McFadden) 5

Married Miss Martha Boyd, to Jas Boyd

March Miss Agnes Crawford to Joe McFadden 2

Died Mrs Lucretia Chambers (July 15th)

Joseph Poag (March) Mack (J D Crawford) Feb

Nancy (Indian) 4

11e Gave April 29th Domestic Missions $4.30
" March 30th Education or Commissions $13.33
All meetings of Session opened and
closed with prayer, and in all cases
a quorum of Members present.

Examined & Approved by Bethel
Presbytery with the recommendation
that the record in future be
more full, April 4th 1856
A. A. James Mod

Register from April 1856 to 1857

July 27th Session met Rev T
W Erwin acting Mod, I W Wellford
asked that his child be Baptized
granted. No business session
adjourned, with prayer by Mod.

Sept 20th Rev Mr Richards Mod.
Session all present. Elders. John S Chambers & Jos H. Crawford ask certificate for themselves and their wives with their servants viz Malden Esther & Cynthia, granted. Also Mrs Agnes J. McFadden asked cert. for self. granted. Mr E. N. Crawford for self and wife to join Bethesda church granted.
Attie (of Agnus) applied. on examination Rec'd. The collection to be taken tomorrow ordered for Bible Society, Had recess untill tomorrow at call of Mod.
21st Morning. Peter Miller on report made by himself ordered to keep back from the Lords table untill session determine by hearing both parties. Recess. Evening. Collection taken & secured thirty dollars to constitute our future Pastor a life member.

J S Tiffany appointed to attend Presbytery.
E R Mills alternate.
adjourned with prayer

Jany 17th 1857. Session met Rev B. L. Beall Mod, Peter (McCullough) asked to be restored. session answered that they think it best for the interests of the Church that he should give further evidence of his repentance. Mr Woodburn applies for certificate of membership for himself & wife. Granted to Mrs Woodburn. but Rumor charging Mr Woodburn with certain unchristian conduct session declined granting cert, untill he should appear and have the charges investigated.
Cynthia (Jeirich McFadden) applied for admission examined; continued for further instruction
After arranging with the Deacons the order for services and the object for collection on tomorrow had recess untill that time.
March 18th Owing to the severity of

the weather session were unable to meet at the time appointed, at last meeting but met to day at the house of Mr Beall by call of Mod; all present.

A communication received from Church Extention Com^tee discussed, and defered. E R Mills appointed to collect the subscriptions to Bethel Female College in our bounds. Roll examined and corrected. The Case of Mr Woodburn called up, and owing to his leaving our bounds with a view to a return this fall session deem it best to defer it untill his return for investigation. B H Stringfellow appointed to attend Presbytery and Mr John Young alternate. Adjourned

March 27th Session met called to order by Mod. Clerk presented the narration & Report with minutes of session for approval, approved, Mrs Malinda Faysoux granted Cert to join Church at Chester C.H. Adjourned.

E R Mills
Clerk

116 Examined & approved Apl 3rd Apl 57
J. G. Richards, Mod

May 1st 1857
Session met and all the members present Rev B.L. Beall as Mod, opened with prayer. Dr S W Douglas applied for admission and on examination was received. Mrs Agnes E McFadden returned her certificate. On motion Session adjourned to meet tomorrow at 10 O'clock.

May 2nd. Session met on adjournment Rev B L Beall Mod all prest, Mary (Drennon) Letty & Malinda (Rader) apply for admission after some conversation were continued. Cynthia (McFadden) came again before session, being examined was received. Collection for F.M. ordered. ~~[illegible]~~

May 31 Session called to order by Moderator all prest except G. H. Nix proceeded to business.

Silas (Neely) (Mike Malinda (Barler) and Mary on being examined were continued for further examination on tomorrow at interval.

Aug 1st Session prest. Mr J Caldwell Boyd applies for admission was examined and continued for further conversation. Silas Lewis (Crawford) Mike Litty Malinda (Rhoda Sicily Sarah) (Mills) appear after some conversation were continued. Esther (McFadden) appeared and confessed the violation of the seventh commandment, professing repentance. The hour for public worship having arrived she was requested by session to keep back from the Lords table on the morrow and allow time for session to consider her case. adjourned untill tomorrow 10 o'clok

Aug 2nd Session met all prest. and opened for business by prayer by Moderator

Joseph Street jr granted certificate to join Ebenezer on his application. J Caldwell Boyd being further examined and session becoming satisfied with his profession recieved him into the communion of the Church. Rhoda, Mike, Litty Malinda & Mary again came before session and on examination Mary (Drennan) was recieved to membership and the others continued. Jack & wife Agnes (Miller) come before session and say that they were members of the Presbyterian Church at Indian town Sumpter Dist but that they had no certificates, and had come for examination with a view to connection with our church. Were examined and recieved. Silas, Lewis, Cicily Sarah; had some conversation with session and the hour for Public worship having arrived session closed for worship.

Sept 25th Session met; Mills absent Miss Menirva Nealy applies for examination was examined & Recieved; to be baptized.

Sept. 26th Session Met opened for business all present. Wm Duncan & wife

Manerva; Rachel A Boyd; J. Caldwell Boyd; asked and were granted Certificates clerk to make particular specifications in that of Rachel A Boyd, as to her absence from our Congregation. Molly Mary Mike Malinda Letty and Rhoda apply for admission were examined but continued.

Esther (McFadden) on her own confession suspended for six months or untill she gives more satisfactory evidences of repentance Mr John Poag with Jas F Whary alternate appointed to attend Presbytery to meet at Pleasant Grove Church, adjourned with prayer.

Sept 27th Session met and opened for business Miss E Moore applies on examination was continued. Misses Mary, Elizabeth & Manerva Farrel apply were examined and continued.

Lewis (Crawford) + Silas (Skelly) again apply and on examination were received, to be baptized adjourned.

Oct. 1857 Session met Mills absent Mrs Mary C Bealle offered a certificate from the Church at Salisbury N.C. which was accepted and she received Miss Elizabeth ~~Bunton~~ Boyd asked for a certificate to move West. and it was granted.

Jany 9th 1858

Session met and opened for business. Mrs E K Mills offered certificate from Bethesda Church accepted and she received Mike Letty Malinda Molly Rhoda Milly (Crawford) apply and on examination Malinda (Rader) and Molly (McCollough) were received the others continued Mary Jane (Eck Crawford) appears confessing the violation of the 7th commandment professing repentance. And on examining her session thought best to suspend her untill she gave better evidences of her sincerity and faith

121

Mr Woodburn having returned to our bounds a communication was received from him stating his inability to meet the session to day and that he wished to return West soon asked a dismission, confessing that he had drank more than he should have done asked forgiveness professing repentance, denying the truth of other rumors. Session having no evidence against him to substantiate the reports charged on motion granted a certificate to join the church in whose bounds he might have his future home.

No further business session adjourned

Feb 21st Session met opened with prayer Mills absent J H Neely appointed clerk pro tem Letty (Rader) applies for admission on examination was received.

Mr Craig with Mr Stringfellow alternate were appointed to attend Presbytery to meet at Zion Church. adjourned

March 28th 1858

Session met at Union church Members all present opened by prayer for business, Clerk read the minutes of session for the year ending April 1st 1858, which on motion were deferred for final action untill session should meet next Sabbath at Fishing Creek church at 10 o'clock A.M.

On Motion adjourned

April 3rd 1858 Session met and opened for business all prest. Clerk again read the minutes for approval. Mike (Rader) applies and on examination was received into membership: to Baptize.

Mary J (Ed Crawford) appeared asking forgiveness for her sin professing repentance. after examination session thought best that she be continued under suspension and is ordered. On Motion the minutes of session as read were approved and ordered to be sent to Presbytery by Mr Stringfellow. On Motion adjourned

E R Sills clerk ses

Examined & approved by Bethel Presbytery at its Sessions at Zion church April 5th 1858.

S. L. Watson Mod Bethel Presᵗ

April 11th 1858 Session met opened for business. Mr Stringfellow delegate to Presbytery reported his attendance, and that there were some recommendations to the churches that would better appear from the printed Minutes of Presbytery. Report approved Lilly (J D Crawford) asked to have her grand child Baptized; granted. Melinda (J D Crawford) hers also; granted. Charlotte (Givens) applyed for admission. Continued Mr Mills appointed to request Mary (Crawford) and Sidney (Miller) to answer session on the charge of the violation of the 7th Commandment, on this day two weeks. Adjourned.

April 28th Session met and constituted R. H. Stringfellow absent. Sidney (Miller) Confessed the charge. and was conversed with and examined by vote suspended for six months or untill satisfactory evidence of her repentance is given. Mrs Harriet P Wallace asked for certificate and dismissal granted.

Mary (Cranford) not being cited the case was continued
May 14th Session met, constituted. Eliza charged by rumor with theft reported. Miss Elizabeth Moore on examination was received a member. had recess untill recess tomorrow. May 15th Session resumed business. Miss Petience Stringfellow examined and received. Milly & Rhoda examined & continued. Mary (Ed Cranford) examined and communed with. Andy Miller asked to have his children baptized granted. Named Johnathan, Martha Ann, & Rhosanna. Recess untill tomorrow 10 oclock.
May 16th All present, resumed business. Charlotte (Grimes) examined & continued, Eliza (McFadden) appeared and denyed the charge. not been proved was cautioned and dismissed. Adjourned,
July 18th Mrs McElroy & Miss Emily McElroy applied for certificate. granted. Lucinda (Neely) applied to be restored having been absent some years. Nancy George (an Indian) examined & continued, Peter (McCollough) asked to have child Baptized granted named Thomas Hay

Sept 24th Session met & constituted. Nancy Bee applied on examination Received. To be Baptized. Mrs D E Willford asked to Baptize her child, granted. Married Sarah Ann
Mr Whorry was appointed delegate to Presbytery. Mr G W Neely alternate, Mills delegate to Synod Mr Pogg alternate Had recess untill 10 o'clock tom
Sept 25th Session resumed business RH Stay filled absent Mills presented a Certificate from Ebenezer for Mena (E R Mills) which was considered and received Mrs Martha E Ross asked for certificate to join Pear Grove church granted. Violet (Rudes) examined and Continued. Recess untill Tomorrow 10 o
Sept 26th Session resumed business all present. Sidney (Mills) appears asking to be restored, was conversed with request not granted. Milly Rhoda & Louisa apply for admission on examination Milly (Stanford) Rhoa (Mills) were received Louisa (Continued
Session met & constituted Mr Neely reported his attendance at Presbytery and in view of necessary and contingent [illegible] Mr Moved [illegible]

and it was Resolved that a collection be taken up annualy on the 2nd Sabbath in Nov for the supply of this fund in our church, Resolved that in future so much of this fund as may be necessary be applied to the expences of delegate to Synod & Presbytery.

D R Mills Reported that owing to his having business in court he could not attend the meeting of Synod. Jany 15th 1839

Session met and organised all prest on Motion of G H Neely Resolved that we dispense with the use of tokens tomorrow. E B Miles offered a certificate from Pleasant Grove church for Abr & Esther servants of Druett Wylie which were recieved adjourned till 11 oclock tomorrow. Jany 16th Session met called to order Sidney (Miller) asks to be restored, examined and refused,

Jany 30th Unity church session met & Mrs Adaline P. Atkinson was examined and recieved to be Baptised, G H Neely clerk protem

March 6th session met all prest organised S. J. Wherry appointed delegate to Presbytery G H Neely alternate.

March 13th Session met

constituted Dr. W. H. Stringfellow

asked certificate and dismissal

granted, and clerk ordered to furnish

him the proper papers Jos. F. Thom[illegible]

clerk of session

March 27th Session met, R. H.

Stringfellow absent, constituted

Louisa (Wm) applied on exam

ination received, to Baptizing.

May (J. D. Crawford) charged with

adultery and refusing to appear ordered

that the clerk cite her to appear

for trial on the 2nd Sabbath in April.

Minutes read and approved

narration read and ordered to be

sent up to Presbytery.

Adjourned with prayer

E. R. Mills

Clerk

[illegible] approval to this page (121) [illegible]

[illegible] the records are too concise [illegible]

distinguished as [illegible] on the [illegible]

[illegible] & to get a new

larger & better session book Approved April 5th 1857

J. A. Davies, Mod.

128 Decem.r 12 1776

Wm Neelly
Margt
Jean
Elizabeth
Mary
[illegible]
Willm
Samuel } Chn

Peter Culley
Elizabeth

Hugh
Margt } Whiteside
Jon
Jas } Chn
Thos

Samuel
Sarah
Thos
Mary } Neelly
Margaret
Elizabeth
2 [illegible] } Chn

Andr
Ann
Willm
Elizabeth
[illegible]
Thos } mcCance
Margaret
Charles
Martha } Children
Jennet
Ann

Math
Mary } Neelly
Thos [illegible]
Dorcas

Hugh
Elizabeth } White
Thos
Margt & Children

Thos
Martha } Ferrel

Robert Neelly

Decr. 13 1776 —
Jn. McDoon

Jn. Jack
Jas. Armstrong

John } Martha } Work

Mary
Robert
John
Margart. } Chil.

Saml. Luck
Saml. Porter
Mary

Robert } Jean } Jack

Jas.
Ann
Robt. Chil.
Andrew

Hugh McLellan
Elizh.
Jean
Jas. Ch.
Agnes

Samuel } Mary } Luck
Elizh. } Elliner } Chil.

David } Agnes } Nelly

Dec 14
Robt } Harper
Margt }

Willm } McCean
Susanna }

David
Willm Chn

Dec 19
Samuel } Cherry
Darkus }

John Silliman

James } Brice
Rosanna }

Robt } Gill
Elinor }
John
Thos
Jas
Archd
Mary
Elinor Chn

James } Gill
Mary }
Mary
Rosanna
Catharine
Jas
Thos Chn

Jany 16 1775
Jona } Jones
Barsheba }
Zuby
John Chn

Jennet McGaughey

Agnis Sharp } Chn
Thomas Clark }

James McGaughey
Jenny

David } Morrow
Mary }
Robert
Jane
Mary
Sarah Chn

John
Mary } Morris

David
Margaret } Boyd

John Ch.
Wm
Wm Nelson

Christ.
Mary } Wright

Margaret
George

John
Sarah } Gill

Thos
Rachel

Jas
George Ch.
Robt

Jas
Elizabeth } Ferguson

John Gill
Nancy

John
Margaret } Miller
Elizabeth
Mary Ann

Jany 18
Wm Craig
Margt
Mary Ch.

John Knox
Eliza
John
Hugh
Wm morton
David
John
Wm

Jas
Martha } Lamond
Robert
Jennet Ch.

Timothy Jones } Clinton
Elinor
Willm
Jean
James

Jos.h } Gaston
Martha
Jean Anderson
Margaret Gaston

John Porter
Kesia
James
Ann
Willm

Jean
Margaret Chn
Susanna

George } Cray
Mary

Mary McClure
James
John
Martha
Hugh
Margaret } R. McClury

Jams } Kn...
Eliza
John
Willm
Saml
Robt
Elizth
Margaret Ch
Agnes

Robt } Gaston
Jennet
Jane
Margaret Chn
Alex.r

Robt } Walker
Jane
Easter
Agnes Chn
Elizth
Martha Mitchell
Robt Henderson

Thos.
Hannah } Garrot
Mary Mullen

John
Peter } Vince
Sally Ringol Clue

Mar.
Esther } Walker

Nicol
Daniel } Chn.

Philip
Rebecka } Walker

John
Catharine } Adams

Peter Nance
Elizabeth
Willm.
Patty
John
Sarah

Martha
Jennet
Elizt.
Mary

Jan 7 30
Archd.
Sarah } Elliot
Willm.
Sarah
Ann
James
Archd. Chn.

Thos.
Sarah } Stone

David
Ann } Henderson

John Walker

Samuel
Jennet } Lard

John } Little
Elizab.
John
Prudence
Willm
Robt Chn
Jane

Philip } Walker
Jennet
John
Margaret
Philip
Thos
Charine
Ann Ch
Ebenezer
Esther

Walter } Brown
Margt
John
Jennet

Elijah } Davis
Elizabth

Jany 31
Willm } Gaston
Jennet

Samuel } McCollough
Margaret

Daniel } Elliot
Elizabeth
Margt
Willm
Andw Forgason
Benjamin
Daniel

Henry } Bishop
Elizabth

James } Duglis
Rosanna
Robt
Mary
James
Wm Lewis

Alexr. } Rosbrough
Martha }
Willm
Margaret

Nicholas } Bishop
Hannah }
Darkis
Hannah
Willm
James
Nicholas
John

Toby &
Hanah mcFadden Wdo
Chatharine } Ch
Ralph }

Edward } mcFadden
Jane }

John mcFadden
George Kelsey
Wm. Ellist

Jas. } Ferguson
Agnes }
Abm
Saml.
Joseph
Betty
Robt
Nonen
Agnis

Willm } mcFadden
Ann }
John Ch

Robt } Martin
Sarah }

Willm } Wiley
Elizth }
Elizth } Ch
Andrew }

T. 6. 7

John } Jo Gaston
Esther }
Robt
Hugh
Deborah
Ebenezer
Esther
Joseph

Isaac McCrary } &c
Margaret Crearie }

John } Gaston
Jennet }

James } Crawford &c
Margt
Martha

Allen } Crawford
Elizabeth }

James } Crawford Jun
Isabel }
William Henderson

Catharine White
John
Thos
Agnes

John } Wiley
Margt }

James } Gaston
Margt }

John } White
Elizabth }

Thos } Walker
Jane }
Allen
Robt

James } Neely
Martha }
George
Margart
Thos
Isaac

Thos } Wilson
Jane }

Willm } Miller
Winnyford }

John } Wilkins
Phebe }
Richd
Samuel
Mary
Willm Creath
Jane
Elizath
Willm
Nancy

Rebecca Gilbrens
Rebecca Jr
Jane
Willm

John } [illegible]
Jane }

Henery } Culp
Barbara }

Augustine } Culp
Agnes }

Willm } Jones McKinney
Barbara }
John
Willm
Hannah

Michael } [illegible]
Mary Barbara }

Bernard } White
Elizath }

John Lockard
Ann White
Robt
Edward

Andrew } Lockard
Mary }

Benjamin
Darkus } Culls

John
Martha } Fleming

John
Ann } Walker
Alex^r
Jane

Mat^w
Rebekah } Patton
Alex^r &
James Courtney

Robt
Sara } Patton
Jane
Jno &
James
Willm ~~[illegible]~~ Simpson
John Barnit

James
Mary } Curry

Ja^s
Jane } Patton &c
Margaret

Willm
Eliz^h } Simpson

Willm
Martha } Brackit

Willm
Mary } Jarvis
Thos

Thos
Jane } Farrel

Machael
Jane } Patton
Mary

Willm
Mary } Hamilton

John
Jennet } Glamory

June 5.

Isaac } Smith
& Mary }

Prudence } Patten

Edward
Elizab.
Phebe } Ch.
John

John } Smith
& Mary }

Jas.
Thos.
Prudence } Ch.
Jacob
John Wiley

James } Smith
Willis }
Jane Ch.
Agnis m. Janett

Patrick } Hamilton
Ellinor }
Jannet } Ch.
May }
Jane Bell

Jeremiah } Claton
Francis }

Augustin
Ann

John } McHenry
Susana }

John
Rebecca
Willm
Mary Ch.
~~Catherine~~

Samuel } Hamilton
Lillis }
Saml.
Agnis Ch.

James
Samuel } Kelso
Susanah

George
Jenet
Elizabeth
Isabel
Sam[l]
Mary Cr
John
Mary Gaston

Jenet McGee

Robt. } Cooper
Jennet
Robt. Gill

Willm } Boyd
Ann
Molly
Ann
Mary

Charles } Strong
Jennet
Martha
Jennet
Chris
Letitia 1 Mary

Alexr } Brown
Agnes
Mary henry
Agnes henry
John Brown
Saml Brown
Alexr Brown Junr
Jennet Brown Cr

John Cannon
Jo Barr

CEMETERY ROSTER

ROW 1

GREEN GILL JORDAN, Born Oct. 12, 1866, Died Mar. 13, 1932.

Mrs. ANNIE DELLA WYLIE JORDAN, Wife of Green Gill, Born May 4, 1877, Died Jan. 17, 1960.

JEWELL A. TURNER HAMBRIGHT, Born Aug. 10, 1913, Died Nov. 14, 1958.

SAMUEL J. LEWIS, Born Jan. 7, 1833, Died Oct. 6, 1917. CSA.

ELIZA STINSON LEWIS, Wife of Samuel J., Born Dec. 6, 1830, Died April 14, 1898.

DANIEL GREEN LEWIS, Born Dec. 12, 1870, Died Mar. 16, 1898.

ROBERT SAMUEL LEWIS, Born May 28, 1869, Died Aug. 6, 1891.

JOSEPH WALTER LEWIS, Born Feb. 23, 1859, Died April 14, 1878.

WILLIE STINSON LEWIS, Born Aug. 28, 1867, Died Oct. 24, 1870.

J. P. C. BOYD, Born Nov. 5, 1861, Died Sept. 16, 1905.

R. B. McFADDEN, Born Dec. 11, 1817, Died June 4, 1889.

MARTHA E. McFADDEN, Wife of R. B., Born Oct. 3, 1820, Died Mar. 28, 1900.

MARY MILLS COOK, Born Dec. 28, 1850, Died June 23, 1893.

J. NEWTON L. COOK, Born Aug. 17, 1852, Died Nov. 21, 1918.

JAMES CRAWFORD COOK, Born Dec. 25, 1881, Died Feb. 18, 1911.

MARTHA C. MOROSO, Born Jan. 1, 1877, Died Feb. 1, 1920.

MARY LENA LOWRY, Born April 6, 1871, Died April 7, 1941.

ELIZABETH DUNLAP, Born Oct. 5, 1796, Died May 5, 1895.

CATHERINE J. DUNLAP, Died Oct. 8, 1893, aged 61 years, 11 months & 15 days.

ELIZABETH NEELY, Born Dec. 9, 1821, Died Jan. 6, 1888.

CECIL MARTIN, Born Oct. 5, 1894, Died Dec. 30, 1895.

L. A. CAMP, Husband of Ellen, Born June 14, 1828, Died July 28, 1896.

ELLEN CAMP, Wife of L. A., Born July 11, 1833, Died Aug. 5, 1904.

CECIL MARTIN SIMS, Son of William & Harriet C., Born Oct. 5, 1894, Died Dec. 30, 1895.

WILLIAM T. SIMS, Born May 11, 1873, Died Dec. 22, 1939.

HARRIET CAMP SIMS, Wife of William, Born Mar. 10, 1872, Died Aug. 10, 1956.

ROW 2

MARION DAVID ALLEN, Born April 15, 1851, Died Feb. 15, 1903.

FRANK HICKLIN, Born April 8, 1889, Died Oct. 1, 1963.

WALTER BROWN McCALLA, Son of Richard & Margaret E., Born Feb. 11, 1859, Died Oct. 10, 1863.

H. VOL. S. GIBBES, Son of H. S. & J. McCalla Gibbes, Born Sept. 12, 18–.

JOHN BROWN LEWIS, Son of Samuel J. & Eliza C., Died July 4, 1860, aged 4 months & 20 days.

ISAIAH W. LEWIS, Born July 2, 1825, Died Dec. 21, 1846.

SAMUEL LEWIS, Born Nov. 2, 1782, Died July 6, 1832.

NARCISSA GASTON LEWIS, Wife of Samuel, Born Nov. 17, 1792, Died Aug. 22, 1871.

SMITH L. LEWIS, Born Aug. 28, 1806, Died May 8, 1860.

JOSEPH STANHOPE LEWIS, Son of Samuel, Died Oct. 20, 1822, aged 2 years, 38 days.

MARTHA M. LEWIS, Born Feb. 10, 1828, Died Aug. 9, 1829.

JAMES M. POAG, Born July 20, 1818, Died April 7, 1865.

MARGARET M. POAG, Died Feb. 17, 1847, aged 30 years.

JOSEPH STEELE, Born Mar. 19, 1789, Died Feb. 9, 1881.

WILLIAM BRADFORD, Died Jan. 22, 1827, in his 56th year.

SARAH BRADFORD, Died Jan. 13, 1827, in her 58th year.

JOSEPH MORROW, Died Oct. 20, 1835, in his 75th year. A Revolutionary soldier, severely wounded at the battle of Hanging Rock.

JANE L. WYLIE, Daughter of S. & J., Died May 5, 1830, aged 1 year & 7 months.

MARY LEWIS, Died May 23, 1819, aged 41 years.

SARAH ELIZABETH JANE MILLEN, Daughter of Robert & Nancy, Died May 28, 1860, aged 1 year, 6 months & 1 day.

NANCY MILLEN, Wife of Robert, Born Dec. 28, 1818, Died Aug. 19, 1875.

ROBERT MILLEN, Died Mar. 10, 1860, aged 60 years, 2 months & 18 days.

JANE MILLEN, 2d Wife of Robert, Died Jan. 4, 1850, aged 37 years, 9 months & 2 days.

JOSEPH ELI MILLEN, Son of Robert & Jane, Died Sept. 7, 1849, aged 3 years.

JANE M. MILLEN, Left Husband & Two Small Children, Died Mar. 11, 1827, in her 28th year.

JAMES R. MILLEN, Died Sept. 8, 1842, aged 8 years, 7 months & 16 days.

DAVID H. MILLEN, Died Mar. 6, 1843, aged 1 year, 11 months & 12 days.

Infant MILLEN, Son of Robert & Janet, Died Feb. 16, 1845, aged 13 days.

MARY WHERRY, Died Dec. 25, 1836, aged 22 years.

JOHN WHERRY, Died Feb. 15, 1836, aged 55 years.

CHARLES M. BRENT, Died Aug. 7, 1838, aged 15 years, 6 months, & 21 days.

ALEXANDER CRAWFORD, Born Mar. 6, 1783, Died Feb. 2, 1851, aged 67 years & 10 months. An Elder of Fishing Creek Church.

Infant WILFONG, Son of D. E. & Susan I., Born April 9, 1859.

ADLINE C. WILFONG, Born July 20, 1858, Died Oct. 14, 1858.

SUSAN I. WILFONG, Born July 20, 1858, Died March 21, 1859.

ROW 2A

ROSANNAH STEELE, Died Aug. 16, 1839, aged 49 years.

JAMES H. STEELE, Died April 19, 1824, aged 10 years.

ROBERT H. STEELE, Died April 23, 1825, aged 6 years.

WILLIAM M. STEELE, Died Jan. 6, 1845, aged 13 years.

DEBORAH WORKMAN, Died Aug. 23, 1830, aged 44 years.

MARY W. WORKMAN, Died Mar. 19, 1843, aged 22 years.

JAMES S. WORKMAN, Died July 22, 1863, aged 80 years.

ISABELLA McMASTER MILLEN, Wife of John, Born April 14, 1821, Died Oct. 7, 1893.

JOHN MILLEN, Born Sept. 21, 1803, Died June 18, 1870.

GEORGE McMASTER MILLEN, Son of John & Isabella, Died Oct. 8, 1867, aged 2 years, 3 months & 12 days.

BARBARA ISABELLA MILLEN, Daughter of John & M. Matilda, Born Feb. 6, 1833, Died Oct. 20, 1860.

HUGH HENRY MILLEN, Son of John & Isabella, Born Sept. 1, 1853, Died Oct. 13, 1853.

MARTHA MATILDA MILLEN, Died Dec. 23, 1843, aged 32 years, 11 months & 23 days.

MARTHA M. MILLEN, Died Oct. 6, 1829, aged 21 years, 1 month & 9 days.

LOUISE JANE MILLEN, Eldest Daughter of John & Matilda, Born Oct. 20, 1835, Died Mar. 31, 1842.

WILLIAM HARVEY MILLEN, Son of John & Matilda, Born Dec. 28, 1831, Died April 17, 1842.

DAVID SAMUEL MILLEN, Son of John & Matilda, Born Jan. 29, 1841, Died Aug. 11, 1842.

PETER W. STRAIT, Born July 19, 1838, Died May 25, 1846.

LEONARD L. STRAIT, Born Oct. 27, 1842, Died May 3, 1844.

ANNAH STRAIT, Born May 5, 1836, Died Sept. 17, 1844.

MARY T. WHERRY, Died Nov. 17, 1843, aged 36 years & 9 months.

SARAH WHERRY, Died Oct. 7, 1843, aged 68 years & 9 months.

R. G. WALLACE, Born May 25, 1837, Died Dec. 10, 1864.

TANDY STULTZ, Born Mar. 7, 1831, Died May 30, 1858.

MARY JANE REID, Wife of Agustine, Born Sept. 11, 1838, Died May 23, 1914.

MARY SPAIN, Wife of G. W. Reid, Born May 6, 1850, Died May 6, 1880.

ROW 3

MARGARET A. STRAIT, Mother, Born May 10, 1841, Died Oct. 22, 1915.

MAGGIE A. STRAIT ALLEN, Wife of J. F., Born Nov. 2, 1874, Died May 13, 1902.

HARRY E. HICKLIN, Born Aug. 8, 1893, Died Feb. 27, 1955.

ADALINE J. BRADFORD, Died Aug. 28, 1854, aged 21 years, 4 months & 7 days.

JOSEPH GASTON, Died April 21, 1823, aged 84 years.

JAMES GASTON, Died July 3, 1825, aged 48 years.

MARTHA GASTON, Died Mar. 4, 1826, aged 86 years.

JANE D. GASTON, Died 1827, in her 18th year.

WILLIAM LEWIS, SEN., Born Feb. 9, 1777, Died Nov. 19, 1822.

WILLIAM LEWIS, SEN., Born Mar. 15, 1746, Died Mar. 4, 1830.

MARGARET LEWIS, Born Dec. 26, 1745, Died Feb. 23, 1834.

JANE MILLER LEWIS, Wife of Col. Joseph Lewis, Born Aug. 18, 1796, Died Nov. 5, 1876.

JOHN JOSEPH McFADDEN, Son of Robert B. & Martha E., Born Nov. 11, 1858, Died Sept. 14, 1863.

Col. JOSEPH LEWIS, Born Jan. 3, 1789, Died Mar. 3, 1861, aged 72 years, 2 months & 6 days.

KEZIAH H. LEWIS, Consort of Joseph, Died Oct. 5, 1817, in her 31st year.

WILLIAM A. LEWIS, Died Oct. 29, 1822, aged 2 years & 26 days.

ANNA J. GASTON, Died Sept. 17, 1841, aged 4 years, 3 months & 24 days.

FLORAH BURNS, Relict of John, Died Aug. 3, 1834, aged 38 years.

WILLIAM WILSON, Son of J. M. K., Died ------ 29, 1816, aged 1 year.

ROBERT BRADFORD, Died April 18, 1823, aged 27 years.

MARY C. DIXON, Wife of Thomas P., Died April 16, 1873, aged 71 years & 4 months.

ALBERT H. NUNNERY, Son of A. L. & E. J., Died Jan. 10, 1870, aged 3 years, 2 months & 11 days.

J. F. STRAIT, Born Sept. 19, 1802, Died July 10, 1865.

GEORGE STRAIT, SR., Died Dec. 9, 1843, aged 79 years & 9 days.

MARY K. M. ROSBOROUGH, Wife of William A., Born July 23, 1817, Died Oct. 28, 1841.

JAMES STRAIT, JR., Died Aug. 23, 1835, in his 41st year.

ELIZABETH STRAIT, Died Feb. 2, 1835, in her 65th year.

LEONARD STRAIT, Died July 25, 1841, aged 16 years.

LEONARD STRAIT, Died Nov. 3, 1825, aged 52 years & 6 days.

SARAH STRAIT, Died June 30, 1833, aged 53 years.

JAMES STRAIT, Died ----- , aged 60 years & 8 months.

MARTHA E. DIXON, Died Dec. 27, 1835, in the 6th year of her age.

ELIZABETH W. DIXON, Died July 16, 1837, in her 32 year.

SARAH A. DIXON, Born March 19, 1832, Died Oct. 14, 1844.

OLIVER PERRY McCULLOCH, Born Dec. 5, 1813, Died Mar. 20, 1870.

SARAH McCULLOCH, Born Oct. 28, 1773, Died Nov. 15, 1844.

MARY McLURE, Wife of James, Born Oct. 9, 1788, Died July 24, 1865.

Captain JAMES McCLURE, Born Sept. 19, 1787, Died Oct. 7, 1855. aged 68 years & 19 days. He led one of the Chester Volunteer Companies to Camp in the War of 1812. He had by inheritance a right to be a patriot being the nephew of Capt. John McClure, who fell at the battle of Hanging Rock in the War of the Revolution.

SARAH McLUER, Daughter of Hugh & Margaret, Born Sept. 14, 1833, Died Mar. 1848, aged 14 years, 6 months & 11 days.

MARY B. McLURE, Born June 30, 1831, Died Sept. 11, 1850.

ROW 4

MARY JANE MILLS, Wife of E. R. & Daughter of James D. & M. D. Crawford, Born Aug. 1, 1827, Died Mar. 22, 1854.

MARTHA M. L. STRAIT, Born April 10, 1831, Died Aug. 4, 1852.

JOHN BOYD, ESQR., Died May 10, 1827, aged 46 years.

WILLIAM A. BOYD, Died Sept. 2, 1824, aged 8 years.

JAMES M. BOYD, Died Oct. 15, 1822, aged 12 years.

CHARLES H. BART, son of L. A. & A. M., Born May 17, 1895, Died Aug. 4, 1909.

SARAH WORKMAN, Born Dec. 13, 1824, Died June 6, 1845.

NANCY H. PORTER, Consort of William, Died Dec. 5, 1844, aged 62 years.

JANE REBECCA WALKER, Consort of Dr. John A., Died Mar. 23, 1847, in her 23d year.

WILLIAM PERRY GILL, 1817-1890. Major, 3d S. C. Regt., CSA, Co. B, 6th Regt. Remains of his wife lie at Uriel.

ROBERT GILL, Born Mar. 4, 1783, Died Dec. 4, 1856, aged 73 years & 9 months.

ELEANOR GILL, Consort of Robert, Died Aug. 4, 1836, in her 49th year.

Infant GILL, Son of William J. & Nancy H., Died June 27, 1851.

NANCY GILL, Died Oct. 7, 1824, aged 17 years.

JOHN GILL, Born June 6, 1819, Died July 1820, aged 1 year.

WASHINGTON L. GILL, Born Jan. 1837, Died Aug. 1837, aged 7 months.

SAMUEL McCULLOCH, Born June 14, 1772, Died April 24, 1830.

THOMAS McCULLOCH, Born Sept. 17, 1796, Died Sept. 6, 1827.

ROSA McG. BASKIN, Born Dec. 29, 1811, Died June 5, 1889.

ROW 5

D. C. CRAWFORD, Born Aug. 13, 1811, Died Jan. 11, 1856.

MARY R. CRAWFORD, Born May 10, 1820, Died Nov. 5, 1843.

REBECCA R. CRAWFORD, Born Mar. 4, 1839, Died Sept. 30, 1840.

MARY C. HENKEL, Died July 23, 1820, aged 16 years.

ELIZABETH F. HENKEL, Died Oct. 28, 1827, aged 20 years & 9 days.

WILLIAM H. HENKEL, Died Nov. 5, 1834, aged 5 years & 1 month.

MARGARET D. BRADFORD, Died Dec. 19, 1854, aged 12 years & 6 days.

W. R. BRADFORD, Died Oct. 20, 1846, aged 2 years, & 6 months.

Infant BRADFORD, daughter of James & Jane, Died Oct. 25, 1846, aged 5 days.

LUCINDAH A. BRADFORD, Died April 27, 1833, aged 27 years, & 6 months.

JAMES BRADFORD, Died Dec. 19, 1850, aged 46 years, 3 months, & 22 days.

THOMAS NEELY, Died Nov. 17, 1815, aged 63 years, 3 months & 14 days. An Elder of Fishing Creek Church.

MILTON ABERNATHY, Born Nov. 16, 1817, Died April 21, 1869.

DAVID BOYD, Died May 17, 1810, aged 28 years.

JENNET BOYD, Wife of David, Died July 15, 1808, aged 30 years.

JOHN A. BOYD, Died April 10, 1813, aged 18 years.

ELIZABETH BOYD, Died August 29, 1835, in her 82d year.

JOHN BOYD, Died Nov. 25, 1822, aged 62 years.

WILLIAM BOYD, JNR., Died May 26, 1823, aged 30 years.

DOROTHY CONLEY, Died July 27, 1815, age 65 years.

LOUISA MINERVA BRADLEY, consort of John A., Born April 16, 1817, Died Mar. 10, 1840.

ISABELLA SMITH, Wife of J. A., Died Sept. 17, 1859, aged 47 years.

JOHN B. REID, Born Jan. 24, 1831, Died May 30, 1861. Co. A, 6th S. C. Vols. CSA.

RACHEL A. REID, Wife of George, Born Sept. 20, 1812, Died Oct. 28, 1868.

ROW 6

JAMES C. McFADDEN, Born May 3, 1858, Died April 8, 1942.

MARY R. McFADDEN, Born Oct. 31, 1859, Died Oct. 9, 1946.

EDNA JAMES McFADDEN, Born April 23, 1897, Died Nov. 14, 1897.

ROBERT A. CRAWFORD, Born Jan. 10, 1826, Died Jan. 4, 1904.

EDWARD CRAWFORD, Born Jan. 25, 1770, Died April 28, 1845.

JANE CRAWFORD, Born June 28, 1774, Died Oct. 22, 1841.

JOHN H. CRAWFORD, Born Nov. 7, 1816, Died Sept. 9, 1853.

EDWARD A. CRAWFORD, Born Nov. 9, 1808, Died Sept. 26, 1832.

GEORGE J. D. CRAWFORD, Born Mar. 24, 1806, Died Mar. 22, 1822.

JAMES D. CRAWFORD, Born Jan. 15, 1798, Died May 28, 1866.

MARY D. CRAWFORD, Wife of James D., Born Jan. 20, 1803, Died Sept. 30, 1894.

SARAH JOHNSTON, Consort of John, Died June 2, 1835, aged 84 years.

JOHN JOHNSTON, SENR., Died Aug. 24, 1820, aged 54 years.

Mrs. MARY GILL, Died Nov. 10, 1816, in her 22d year.

AGNESS GILL, Died October 1st 1815, aged 50 years.

ABRAHAM GILL, Died August 20th 1815, in the 50th year of his age.

WILLIAM R. STRAIT, Born Oct. 12, 1809, Died Oct. 14, 1873, aged 64 years & 2 days.

GEORGE GILL STRAIT, Son of John R. & Margaret A., Born Oct. 4, 1866, Died June 22, 1872.

J. R. STRAIT, Born Aug. 25, 1836, Died June 11, 1887.

JOHN B. STRAIT, Born Aug. 30, 1861, Died April 19, 1902.

PETER WYLIE, Died Feb. 19, 1795, aged 84 years.

ANN WYLIE, Wife of Peter, Died June 4, 1783, in her 63d year.

ANN WYLIE, Died Oct. 7, 1797, in her 13th year.

JAMES WYLIE, Died Oct. 13, 1821, in his 28th year.

NANCY JANE C. HARDIN, Daughter of D. N. & Mary K., Died Jan. 3, 1836, aged 1 year, 10 months & 22 days.

MARY K. HARDIN, Consort of D. N., Died Mar. 1, 1839, aged 28 years, 8 months & 20 days.

THOMAS GILL, Died Sept. 29, 1808, in his 64th year.

ROBERT GILL, Died June 30, 1804, aged 84 years.

ELLENOR GILL, Died Dec. 13, 1801, aged 80 years.

DR. ANDREW J. SMITH, Born Aug. 20, 1824, Died Nov. 16, 1852.

MARGARET WORKMAN, Born May 19, 1842, Died July 28, 1848.

JAMES WORKMAN, Died May 3, 1847, aged 52 years.

ROBERT WORKMAN, Died Mar. 22, 1845, aged 42 years.

JOHN WORKMAN, Died Feb. 1, 1845, aged 46 years & 11 months.

MARTHA MARKS, Consort of Augustus C. & Daughter of Robert & Margaret Workman, Died Jan. 18, 1845, aged 43 years.

WILLIAM WORKMAN, Died Sept. 11, 1839, aged 38 years & 11 months.

ROBERT WORKMAN, Born Aug. 1, 1761, Died Jan. 11, 1844.

MARGARET WORKMAN, Consort of Robert, Born Oct. 5, 1765, Died Feb. 12, 1848, aged 82 years, 4 months & 7 days.

ROBERT S. ROACH, Born Sept. 22, 1867, Died Nov. 2, 1868.

GEORGE R. ROACH, Son of T. J. & S. A., Born Aug. 23, 1873, Died Sept. 21, 1876.

MARY A. ROACH, Daughter of T. J. & S. A., Born Feb. 5, 1869, Died Sept. 5, 1876.

J. LORAINE ROACH, Son of T. J. & S. A., Born Nov. 7, 1884, Died June 7, 1885.

AGNES L. ROACH, Daughter of T. J. & S. A., Born Dec. 5, 1870, Died Sept. 24, 1876.

BOYD, Infant Son, Died Oct. 10, 1890.

FRANCIS BOYD, Died Feb. 29, 1816, aged 33 years.

DAVID BOYD, SR., Died May 11, 1815, aged 77 years.

ROW 7

LEROY BUFORD, Died Dec. 16, 1810, aged 60 years.

MARY BUFORD DAVIES, Wife of Revd. John B., Died July 30, 1854, aged 75 years.

FRANCES JUNELL DAVIES, Died April 3, 1804, aged 40 days.

ALLEN SIMPSON, Died Oct. 1790, aged 14 months.

Infant DAVIES, Son of John B. & Mary, Born dead Sept. 2, 1798.

JANET WALKER, Died Dec. 12, 1790, aged 80 years.

JOHN WALKER, Died Oct. 24, 1802, aged 75 years.

JOHN WALKER, Died June 16, 1792, aged 37 years.

Infant WALKER, Son of William & Jane, Died Jan. 31, 1801, aged 5 weeks.

SALLY LAMIRA KELSEY, Daughter of John & Sarah, Died Sept. 7, 1827, aged 3 years, 3 months & 23 days.

SARAH BOYD, Died Sept. 23, 1835, in her 51 year.

Capt. ROBT. COOPER, Born Decr. 25th 1746 and departed this life May the 15th 1799 [1798] aged 53 [52] years. A Revolutionary character and active member of society.

JOHN COOPER, 1751-1804. Pvt., Col. E. Lacey's Regt., S. C. Militia, Rev. War.

ELIZABETH S. HARTNESS, Died April 14th 1816.

"Here truth and sense & beauty sleep
Here every virtue lies
Her husband and her children weep
Though she has reached the skies."

Colo. ARCHD. GILL of the 11th Regiment of Militia who died 12th October 1803, aged 46 years, and his two wives CATHERINE and AGNES.

ISABELLA GILL, Died Oct. 5, 1834, aged 42 years.

CHARLOTTE C. PAGAN, Died July 15, 1842, aged 16 years & 5 months.

CHARLOTTE L. PAGAN, Daughter of John M., Died Aug. 2, 1844, aged 1 year, 10 months & 20 days.

MARY PAGAN, Born April 20, 1789, Died March 10, 1852.

JAMES STEWART McCARLEY, Son of J. A., Born July 4, 1877, Died Aug. 6, 1887.

ROW 8

Infant McCARLEY, Son of J. A., aged 3 days.

ALEXANDER McCARLEY, Son of J. A., Born Nov. 14, 1881, Died Jan. 3, 1888.

AUGUSTA M. SAYE – 1869 - 1949

JOE M. SAYE – 1894 - 1932

JAMES McJUNKIN SAYE, Born Jan. 21, 1854, Died July 19, 1915.

JOSEPH THEODORE DUSENBURY, Son of Charles & Rosa, Born Oct. 1, 1890, Died Sept. 26, 1892.

Rev. JAMES H. SAYE, Born Jan. 29, 1808, Died Nov. 20, 1892.

REBECCA SAYE, Wife of Rev. James H., Born May 11, 1818, Died April 6, 1904.

JOHN W. SAYE, Son of Rev. James H. & Rebecca, Born May 17, 1860, Died Aug. 4, 1871.

WILLIAM M. SAYE Son of Rev. James H. & Rebecca, Born July 15, 1858, Union County, S. C., Died May 30, 1884, in Cameron, Texas.

MARGARET JANE MILLEN, Wife of Rev. A. W., Died Mar. 9, 1854, aged 31 years.

WILLIAM STRINGFELLOW, Died May 22, 1849, in his 70th year.

Mrs. PATIENCE STRINGFELLOW, Died Dec. 23, 1843, in her 60th year.

ELIZABETH STRINGFELLOW, Died Feb. 14, 1818, aged 3 years, 7 months & 22 days.

ELIZABETH C. KELSEY, Daughter of T. & M., Born July 11, 1824, Died Oct. 19, 1828.

CHARLES BOYD, Died Oct. 29, 1828, aged 50 years.

JINCY S. M. KELSEY, 2d Daughter of John & Sarah, Died Oct. 3, 1819, aged 5 years & 24 days.

THOMAS KELSEY, Born Oct. 20, 1796, Died Oct. 13, 1828.

ELIZABETH KELSEY, Died June 19, 1824, aged 59 years.

CHRISTOPHER STRAIT, Died Jan. 14, 1816, aged 77 years.

MARY STRIGHT, Wife of Christopher, Died Aug. 29, 1784, in her 48th year.

MARGARET STRIGHT, alias PATON, Wife of Christopher, Died July 18, 1788, in her 35th year.

ROSANNA STRAIT, Wife of Christopher, Died Oct. 2, 1812, aged 46 years.

ROBERT GILL, Died Sept. 24, 1786, in his 33d year.

JOHN ALLAN Died Oct. 17, 1787, aged 56 years.

AGNES CRAWFORD, Wife of James, Died Aug. 14, 1838, aged about 82 years.

SALLY A. PAGAN, Daughter of Alexander, Died Feb. 25, 1858.

A. GILL PAGAN, Born July 13, 1823, Died July 11, 1857, aged 34 years & 1 day.

ROW 9

JAMES PHINNEY, Born Mar. 17, 1807, Died Aug. 7, 1824.

SARAH CULP, Born Nov. 6, 1812, Died April 9, 1902.

E. A. FINNEY, Died at age 63. A Mason.

SAMUEL MILLEN, Born Mar. 15, 1836, Died May 31, 1862. CSA. He was killed at the battle of Seven Pines, Va.

MARTHA MILLEN, Died Feb. 2, 1837, in her 60th year.

JOHN MILLEN, SR., Died July 31, 1844, aged 68 years.

ROBERT MILLEN, Died April 29, 1806, about 60 years of age.

ELIZABETH MILLEN, alias WILLSON, Wife of Robert Millen, Died Sept. 2, 1785, aged 72 years.

ELIZABETH WILSON, alias MILLS, Died Nov. 18, 1797.

Infant MILLEN, Son of William, Died April 30, 1809, aged 6 days.

MARY ANN MILLEN, Died June 27, 1822, aged 17 years & 5 months.

ROBERT MILLEN, Died Jan. 24, 1826, aged 23 years, 3 months & 7 days.

JANE C. KELSEY, Daughter of John & Sarah, Born Oct. 2, 1820, Died Sept. 10, 1854.

ELIZABETH KELSEY, Daughter of John & Sarah, Died Oct. 19, 1828, aged 16 years, 3 months & 12 days.

JAMES FERGUSON, Died Oct. 21, 1778, in the 43d year of his age.
"Remember me as you pass by
As I am now so you must be
Prepare for Death and follow me."

ELEANOR BARR Died Mar. 10, 1813, aged 36 years, 4 months.

ROW 10

JOSEPH GASTON SAYE, Son of James H. & Jean H., Pfc. Co. E, 36th Armored Infantry, 3d Armored Division, World War II, Born June 16, 1925, Died Aug. 1, 1944. Killed in action at St. Lo, Normandy, France.

JAMES HODGE SAYE, Born June 15, 1893, Died Oct. 21, 1971.

E. H. MILLEN, Born Dec. 3, 1842, Died Mar. 30, 1928.

MARIAH L. MILLEN, Wife of E. H., Born May 2, 1837, Died July 6, 1921.

JOHN A. MILLEN, Son of J. A., Born Aug. 17, 1864, Died Sept. 29, 1888.

WILLIE E. MILLEN, Son of E. H. & M. L., Born April 16, 1879, Died Nov. 5, 1883.

Infant MILLEN, Daughter of William, Died Feb. 21, 1804, aged 11 days.

Infant NEELY, Son of Thomas.

ELIZABETH LAMON, Died June 25th 1801, aged 30 years.

JAMES LAMON, Died Sept. 26, 1778, in the 40th year of his age.

JOHN LEWIS, Son of William & Margaret, Died Oct. 24, 1774, aged 4 months & 2 days.

Infant LEWIS, Son of William & Margaret, stillborn Mar. 2, 1779.

BENJAMIN LEWIS, Son of William & Margaret, Died Nov. 14, 1775, aged 1 month & 21 days.

ALEXANDER L. PAGAN, Died Oct. 16, 1817, aged 3 years, 8 months & 10 days.

ROBERT MILLS, Died Oct. 5, 1786, aged 11 months & 5 days.

JAMES R. GILL, Born Oct. 27, 1820, Died Oct. 22, 1821.

Mrs. MARY MILLS, Consort of Col. John Mills, Born Oct. 1758, in the Colony of Pennsylvania, Died Jan. 29, 1841, in the State of South Carolina. A woman of the Revolution. She died in the communion of Fishing Creek Church.

Col. JOHN MILLS, Died Mar. 19, 1795, in his 38th year. A Revolutionary officer.

JOHN MILLS, Died Nov. 9, 1815, aged 83 years.

MARY ANN WILSON, alias MILLS, Died Feb. 3, 1799, aged 36 years.

SARAH LILLY, Wife of James, Died June 4, 1843, in her 59th year.

JOHN M. LILLY, Died April 20, 1820, aged 10 years & 6 months.

Two Infants LILLY.

JOHN MILLS, ESQR., Born Dec. 21, 1791, Died Jan. 31, 1826, Graduate of S. C. College, Dec. 1818, and licensed to practice law Dec. 1819.

JOHN MILLS, Son of R. G. & Prudence S. Mills, Died Dec. 22, 1829, aged 2 years & 9 months.

PRUDENCE SELINA MILLS, Consort of Major Robert G. Mills, Born Sept. 21, 1809, Died Aug. 24, 1841.

SUSANNAH NEELY (headstone broken)

S. H. G. NEELY (headstone broken)

Capt. JAMES A. H. GASTON, Son of Joseph & Jane, Died July 26, 1859, in his 58th year.

JOSEPH GASTON, Born Jan. 22, 1763, Died Oct. 10, 1836, aged 73 years, 8 months & 18 days. "He was a practical Patriot and Christian. A soldier of the Revolution and for many years an Elder in the Presbyterian Church."

JANE GASTON, Wife of Joseph, Born April 10, 1767, Died June 27, 1858, aged 91 years.

WILLIAM NEELY, Born May 7, 1792, Died Feb. 11, 1852, in his 60th year.

ELIZA NEELY, Born Sept. 20, 1794, Died June 7, 1845.

THOMAS NEELY, Died Jan. 19, 1846, aged 27 years.

JAMES H. NEELY, Died at Kinston, N. C., April 23, 1862, in his 23d year of camp fever. Member of Company B, 26th Regt. N. C. Troops, CSA.

ROW 11

JOSEPH S. POAG, Born Nov. 11, 1826, Died Dec. 1, 1849, aged 23 years & 15 days.

THEODORE C. POAG, Son of John & Cynthia, Died April 22, 1825, aged 9 years & 11 months.

D. RANDOLPH POAG, CSA. Born Feb. 6, 1840, Died Sept. 10, 1862, at Warrenton, Va.

ROBERT M. POAG, CSA. Born Oct. 11, 1832, Died Mar. 4, 1864, at Greeneville, Tenn.

MARGARET CARR, Died Mar. 9, 1825.

DAVID CARR, Died May 1805.

MARGARET WORKMAN, Consort of John, Born 1774, Died Feb. 13, 1847.

JANE McLURE, Died Aug. 4, 1838, in her 75th year.

HUGH M'CLUER, Died Mar. 3, 1802, aged 42 years.

JOHN M'CLUER, Died July 20, 1825, aged 30 years.

RICHARD ROWLAND, Died Jan. 10, 1836, aged 1 year, & 9 months.

JENNET KELSO, Sister of Samuel, Died July 30, 1776, aged 66.

SAMUEL KELSO, Died Aug. 16, 1796, aged 76 years.

SUSANNAH KELSO, Mother of John Kelso, Died Sept. 12, 1804, in her 83d year.

JOHN KELSO, Died Sept. 15, 1776, aged 13 years.

ANDERSON M. BOYD, Died Dec. 28, 1841, aged 29 years & 15 days.

JACOB L. BOYD, Died Aug. 12, 1844, aged 23 years, 10 months, & 12 days.

DAVID F. BOYD, Died Aug. 10, 1841, aged 21 years, 4 months, 19 days.

EUGENIUS MILLS, Born Aug. 10, 1836, Died Oct. 12, 1842.

Major ROBERT G. MILLS, Died Feb. 8, 1842, in his 56th year. Member of S. C. State Legislature & State Convention of 1832; elected Superintendent of Public Works.

Major JOHN NEELY, Died Dec. 30, 1832, aged 50 years & 6 months.

MATTHEW JOHNSTON, Died Feb. 16, 1841, aged 51 years.

LUCRETIA JOHNSTON, Daughter of John & Sarah, Born Sept. 6, 1853, Died Sept. 26, 1854.

WILLIAM H. CAMPTON, Born May 6, 1848, Died Nov. 8, 1869.

ROW 12

ESSIE J. ALLEN, Daughter of C. M. & M. E. Allen, Born April 7, 1892 Died Sept. 8, 1894.

Infant ALLEN, Mar. 8, 1897.

GEORGE D. ALLEN Born April 3, 1900 Died Nov. 6, 1900.

CYNTHIA POAG, Wife of John, Died Nov. 24, 1873, in her 63d year.

JOHN POAG, Born Dec. 10, 1784, May 12, 1863. He was a Ruling Elder in Fishing Creek Church about 25 years.

HANNAH POAG, Died June 26, 1830, aged 39 years.

KESIAH E. POAG, Died Sept. 9, 1826, aged 10 years.

LEROY SMITH, Died June 30, 1826, aged 8 months & 18 days.

JAMES SMITH, Died Aug. 1824, aged 4 months & 17 days.

JANE BOYD, Born Mar. 11, 1800, Died Sept. 24, 1846.

WILLIAM BOYD, JR., Died July 28, 1840, aged 48 years.

JAMES L. HEFLEY, Died Aug. 31, 1842, aged 5 years & 14 months.

SARAH BOYD, Died Nov. 5, 1825, aged 34 years.

MARY S. BOYD, Born Aug. 27, 1785, Died Sept. 21, 1823.

J. DANNAN BOYD, Died June 5, 1822, aged 17 months.

HUGH WHITESIDE, ESQR., Died Nov. 10, 1802, aged 64.

JOHN WORKMAN, Died Nov. 11, 1816, aged 48 years.

WILLIAM PORTER, Died Mar. 6, 1779, aged 20½ years.

DAVID PORTER, Died Jan. 8, 1780, aged 3 years.

MARY KELSEY, Wife of Robert, Died May 24, 1774, aged 54 years.

HUGH KELSEY, Died June 18, 1817, in his 63d year.

ROBERT KELSEY, Died July 20, 1789, aged 1 year & 9 months.

CHARLES NEELY, Died Nov. 23, 1832, aged 60.

NANCY NEELY, Died 1837, aged about 90 years.

WILLIAM C. NEELY, Died Aug. 13, 1844, aged 7 years & 4 months.

MARGARET R. M. NEELY, Wife of George H., Born April 2, 1815, Died Mar. 18, 1873, aged 57 years, 11 months & 15 days.

MARGARET E. NEELY, Born Sept. 8, 1846, Died Oct. 6, 1871, aged 25 years & 28 days.

EUGENE DRENNAN, Son of G. A. & S. M., Died at age 2 years & 6 months. Precious Dust.

G. A. DRENNAN, Died Nov. 19, 1885.

ROW 13

DAVID H. MILLER, Died Oct. 9, 1854, aged 34 years, 1 month & 9 days. A Deacon in Fishing Creek Church.

JOHN D. MILLER, Died July 27, 1825, aged 22 years & 16 days.

ROBERT MILLER, Died Dec. 7, 1852, aged 78 years, 1 month & 7 days.

JANE D. MILLER, Wife of Robert, Born Dec. 28, 1778, Died Dec. 14, 1865, aged 87 years.

JANE P. BOYD, Died Dec. 15, 1842, aged 21 years & 8 months.

MARTHA A. BOYD, Died Oct. 28, 1841, aged 6 years, & 11 months.

ELIZABETH A. WOODRUFF, Died Feb. 16, 1811, aged 18 years, 2 months & 22 days.

CHARLES BOYD, SR., Died Sept. 26, 1844 in his 86th year. An Elder of Fishing Creek Presbyterian Church.

SARAH BOYD, Died Mar. 17, 1824, aged 66 years.

MARGARET BOYD, Died Feb. 17, 1816, aged 18 years.

JAMES STEELE, Died Oct. 6, 1811, aged 46 years. An Elder in Fishing Creek Church.

MARY STEELE, Died June 30, 1838, in her 79th year.

ANNIE STEELE, Born Feb. 19, 1798, Died Dec. 12, 1880.

SAMUEL McCANCE, Died Nov. 1792, aged 54 years.

THOMAS WHITE, Born Mar. 5, 1767, Died July 5, 1830, aged 63 years & 4 months.

HUGH WHITE, Died May 13, 1801, aged 64 years.

MARY NEELY, Died Mar. 8, 1849, aged 57 years.

MARGT. McCANCE, alias NEELY, Died Jan. 1772, aged 36 years.

THOMAS J. W. NEELY, Sept. 24, 1814 – Dec. 20, 1853.

CHARLES NEELY, Born Nov. 9, 1775, Died Nov. 23, 1832.

ELENOR NEELY, Died Sept. 25, 1804, Aged 27 years.

ELIZABETH ELENOR NEELY, Daughter of John & Mary C. Neely, Born July 16, 1834, Died Oct. 14, 1838, aged 4 years, 2 months & 28 days.

JOHN M. NEELY, Son of J. & M. C. Neely, Died May 10, 1839, aged 1 year, 5 months & 6 days.

JOHN NEELY, Born June 28, 1801, Died Nov. 9, 1845, aged 42 years, 4 months & 11 days.

JANE S. NEELY, Born July 20, 1806, Died Oct. 9, 1879.

ALEXANDER P. W. NEELY, Born Dec. 17, 1839, Died June 22, 1862. Co. A, 6th S. C. Volunteers, CSA.

JAMES DRENNAN, ESQ., Born May 10, 1795, Died Mar. 31, 1855.

JOHN LOWRY NEELY, Son of John H. & A. L., Born Feb. 4, 1871, Died Aug. 18, 1873.

VICTORIA E. DRENNAN, Daughter of W. R. & J. E., Born Aug. 23, 1864, Died Nov. 1, 1865.

MARY J. DRENNAN, Born Nov. 23, 1852, Died June 23, 1874.

JOHN DRENNAN, Born June 22, 1811, Died April 19, 1855.

ROW 14

MARY L. MILLER, Daughter of Robert & Jane, Died June 9, 1857, aged 50 years.

TEMPERANCE FERGUSON, Died Sept. 3, 1826, aged 24.

ROW 15

MARY McFADDEN NEELY, Wife of J. G. R. Neely, Born Aug. 30, 1852, Died June 7, 1898.

AMELIA CRAWFORD McFADDEN, Wife of James McFadden, Jan. 15, 1833 – July 11, 1916.

JAMES McFADDEN, Born Nov. 6, 1828, Died May 27, 1908.

W. H. McFADDEN, Born Sept. 22, 1877, Died April 22, 1916.

JAMES B. HICKLIN Nov. 20, 1893 – Jan. 14, 1928. Pvt., 15th Aero Constr. Co.

J. S. POAG, Born Mar. 17, 1814, Died Jan. 10, 1845.

MARY H. POAG, Born Oct. 8, 1837, Died Aug. 28, 1855.

CHRISTINE B. HICKLIN, Born Aug. 29, 1846, Died May 4, 1880.

W. C. HICKLIN Jan. 29, 1841 – June 25, 1917. Co. A, 6th S. C. Vols., CSA.

ESTHER P. HICKLIN, Born Jan. 8, 1859, Died Sept. 21, 1898.

ANNA POAG HICKLIN, Born Jan. 9, 1868, Died Aug. 19, 1951.

WILLIAM HENRY NEELY, Died Oct. 3, 1823, aged 13 years, 4 months & 17 days.

MARY A. S. CHAMBERS, Born June 21, 1822, Died Nov. 2, 1828.

LUCRETIA CHAMBERS, Born July 19, 1791, Died July 15, 1855.

WILLIAM CHAMBERS, Born Oct. 23, 1789, Died Dec. 5, 1827.

JOHN CHAMBERS, Born Dec. 15, 1749, Died Sept. 9, 1824.

ELIZABETH CHAMBERS, Wife of John, Born July 17, 1760, Died April 5, 1808.

SARAH NEELY, Died Dec. 28, 1806, aged 75 years.

SAMUEL NEELY, Died Sept. 9, 1803, aged 77 years. One of the first Elders of Fishing Creek Church.

SARAH BROWN, daughter of Joseph & Mary, Died Jan. 10, 1791.

MARY BROWN, alias NEELY, Died Sept. 9, 1779, aged 23 years, & 27 days.

JAMES NEELY, Died October 26, 1804, aged 30 years.

THOMAS LATTA, Born Nov. 1, 1763, Died Nov. 14, 1807, aged 44 years & 13 days.

JEAN WHITE, Died Sept. 24, 1779, aged 3 months.

JAMES WHITE, Son of Hugh & Elizabeth, Died May 9, 1774, aged 1 year & 9 months.

JOHN MILLS KELSEY, Died June 9, 1794, aged 5 months.

JENNET KELSEY, Died Jan. 17, 1786, aged 17 years.

MARY C. HOWELL Born Sept. 2, 1815, Died July 28, 1853.

HANNAH DRENNAN, Died April 29, 1837, aged 57 years.

ROW 16

ALLIE MARIE CARTER, Daughter of W. J. & K. I., Born Nov. 3, 1905, Died May 5, 1907.

Infant HICKLIN, Daughter of J. R. & Susan, Died Sept. 7, 1898.

ANNA J. McDANIEL HICKLIN, 1868-1942.

JAMES C. HICKLIN 1867 - 1929.

JOSEPH H. HICKLIN, Son of James C. & Anna J. 1905 - 1911

HICKLIN, Three Infants of James C. & Anna J., Died 1889, 1898, & 1899.

JAMES E. HICKLIN

JOHN BACKSTROM HICKLIN, Son of W. C. & C. L., Died Oct. 13, 1870, aged 1 year, 2 months & 17 days.

JAMES C. HICKLIN, Died Sept. 1, 1852, aged 37 years, 3 months & 2 days.

R. N. POAG, Wife of J. C. Hicklin, Born Mar. 18, 1820, Died Jan. 11, 1879.

JANE V. HICKLIN June 4, 1843 - Dec. 30, 1860.

JANE POAG, Wife of William, Sr., Born Jan. 31, 1790, Died Oct. 26, 1867.

THOMAS J. POAG, Born Mar. 16, 1832, Died Aug. 22, 1861. Co. A, 6th S. C. Vols., CSA.

WILLIAM M. POAG, CSA. Born May 31, 1822, Died Oct. 17, 1864.

J. EDGAR POAG, 1854 - 1936

ROSEY MARGARET McCLINTOCK, Died Dec. 29, 1799, in her 22d year.

S. A. PARRISH, Born Mar. 22, 1853, Died Dec. 14, 1893.

WILLIAM WHARRY, Died Aug. 21, 1815, aged 3 years.

ELIZABETH N. CHAMBERS, Born Feb. 10, 1818, Died Oct. 3, 1822.

STEWART S. CHAMBERS, Born Oct. 25, 1825, Died April 18, 1827.

SAMUEL NEELY, Son of Samuel & Sarah, Died Sept. 19, 1762, aged 17 years.

THOMAS NEELY, Died Sept. 17, 1793, aged 30 years.

AGNUS DRENNAN, Died Oct. 12, 1783, aged 4 years.

HUGH DRENNAN, Died Mar. 12, 1802, aged 79 years.

MARY DRENNAN, Died Mar. 16, 1801, aged 48 years.

Infant GILL, Son of J. G. B. & E. S., Died Mar. 1, 1841, aged 3 years.

MARY NEELY, Died Feb. 10, 1809, aged 7 years, 5 months & 23 days.

Infant McFADDEN, of John & Sarah, Born April 10, 1845, Died April 26, 1845, aged 16 days.

HUGH DRENNAN, ESQR., Died Nov. 22, 1835, aged 53 years, 8 months & 6 days.

ELEANOR DRENNAN, Died Dec. 1, 1807, aged 32 years, 9 months, & 17 days.

MARGARET DRENNAN, Born Sept. 3, 1782, Died Oct. 23, 1810, aged 58 years, 1 month & 14 days.

WILLIAM DRENNAN, Died July 9, 1845, aged 73 years.

HUGH WALLACE DRENNAN, Son of Harvey H. & Elizabeth, Died Sept. 15, 1848, aged 7 months & 18 days.

JANE DRENNAN, Born Oct. 18, 1774, Died Mar. 12, 1844.

Infant DRENNAN, Son of James & Mary, Died July 1, 1842, aged 4 months.

MARY E. S. J. BROWN, daughter of T. & M. A., Born April 1, 1853, Died June 30, 1853.

AGNES C. DRENNAN, Oct. 23, 1859 - Oct. 22, 1865.

THOMAS CALDWELL, Born Nov. 19, 1850, Died Jan. 20, 1878.

MARY ANN CALDWELL, Daughter of Wm. & Nancy, Born Nov. 9, 1854, Died Sept. 11, 1884.

ROW 17

THOMAS RUPERT STRAIT May 26, 1905 - April 20, 1972.

RUTH IONE STRAIT, Born Dec. 13, 1912, Died April 14, 1931.

SAMUEL STRAIT, Son of S. G., Born Oct. 14, 1906, Died Nov. 3, 1906.

S. G. STRAIT, Born May 20, 1878, Died May 24, 1928.

CORA CONRAD STRAIT, Wife of S. G. Strait, Jan. 1, 1887 - Sept. 15, 1965.

EDWARD M. HICKLIN, Feb. 4, 1892, Jan. 20, 1954.

WINIFRED B. HICKLIN Oct. 8, 1898 - Sept. 22, 1942

JAMES HICKLIN Sept. 22, 1930 - July 19, 1954.

JONAS RADER, Born Mar. 16, 1803, Catawba County, N. C., Died Aug. 5, 1871. For 32 years a member of Fishing Creek Presbyterian Church, and a Ruling Elder for the last 7 years.

SARAH M. RADER, Wife of Jonas, Born May 2, 1816, Died July 20, 1879.

Infant RADER, Daughter of Jonas & Sarah M., Born and Died ------ 21, 1849.

ELI C. RADER, Born Dec. 22, 1840, Died May 24, 1864. Sgt. Co. F, 6th S. C. Vols., CSA. Was mortally wounded at the battle of the Wilderness, May 6, 1864, and died at Verdiersville, Va.

MARTHA P. POAG, Born Nov. 7, 1830, Died Jan. 28, 1903.

LUVICA L. POAG, Born Dec. 11, 1828, Died Oct. 19, 1904.

JOHN NEELY, Died Oct. 1783, aged 61 years.

ELIZABETH NEELY, Died May 4, 1774, aged 33 years.

ROW 18

RALPH BUFORD McFADDEN, Died Jan. 23, 1843, aged 3 years, 6 months & 23 days.

JAMES E. McFADDEN, Died Nov. 14, 1844, aged 60 years, 3 months & 17 days. A Ruling Elder of Fishing Creek Presbyterian Church.

RUFUS D. McFADDEN, Died Oct. 28, 1845, aged 2 years, 5 months & 18 days.

MARGARET J. McFADDEN, Daughter of Ralph & Eliza J., Born Dec. 8, 1852, Died Oct. 20, 1854, aged 1 year, 10 months & 21 days.

Infant McFADDEN, Son.

MARY McFADDEN, Died April 16, 1848, aged 37 years, 4 days.

ISAAC McFADDEN, Born Dec. 5, 1807, Feb. 8, 1855, aged 47 years, 2 months & 3 days.

ELLA GILL McFADDEN, Daughter of James & Amelia, Born Feb. 19, 1871, Died Sept. 28, 1882.

MATTHEW JAMES NEELY, Died Mar. 22, 1847, aged 23 years, 1 month & 28 days.

JANE DUNLAP, Died Sept. 25, 1872, aged 77 years, 6 months & 21 days.

Infant DUNLAP, Son of J. J. & M., Born and died Sept. 30, 1867.

ROBERT P. DUNLAP, Died Sept. 25, 1872, aged 5 months, & 16 days.

JOHN T. NEELY, Died April 21, 1845, aged 8 years, 1 month & 25 days.

ANN DUNLAP, Died Dec. 23, 1861, aged 27 years, 9 months & 5 days.

THADDEUS C. JONES, Died Aug. 9, 1849, aged 30 years.

JONATHAN JONES, Died Aug. 4, 1835, aged 78 years.

MARY DOWNING, Died Mar. 19, 1832, aged 86.

JOHN DOWNING, Died May 1802, aged 62 years.

WILMOT STEWART GIBBES, Born Nov. 16, 1782, Died Sept. 11, 1852.

ALEX. DE SAUSSERE GIBBES, Born July 6, 1822, Died Sept. 4, 1855.

MARY E. DUNLAP, Died Sept. 30, 1872, aged 3 years, 11 months & 15 days.

SIDNEY J. DUNLAP, Died Oct. 31, 1885, aged 3 months & 8 days.

MAMIE BELL DUNLAP, Daughter of W. H. & L. I., Born Jan. 17, 1892, Died May 22, 1893.

Infant DUNLAP, Daughter of W. H. & L. I., Born and died July 23, 1880.

LULA M. DUNLAP, Died Oct. 15, 1892, aged 5 years, 11 months & 8 days.

SAMUEL WHERRY, Died Dec. 26, 1791, in his 57th year.

DORCUS WHARRY, Wife of Samuel, Died Oct. 19, 1810, aged 65 years.

WILLIAM GILMORE, Born Dec. 26, 1783, Died Nov. 9, 1839.

MARY DRENNAN, Born Jan. 1, 1818, Died April 2, 1897.

Infant NEELY, of A. & L. E., Died Oct. 19, 1829, aged 20 days.

MARY NARCISSA NEELY, Daughter of A. & L. E., Died Sept. 18, 1837, aged 3 years, 6 months & 9 days.

AMARYLLIS EMILY GILMORE, Daughter Wm. & Mary, Born Dec. 3, 1824, Died July 23, 1852, aged 27 years, 7 months & 20 days.

HUGH DRENNAN, Born April 12, 1804, Died Sept. 28, 1870.

MARY GILMORE, Wife of William, Born May 29, 1790, Died Sept. 8, 1853, aged 63 years, 3 months & 10 days.

M. ELIZABETH NELSON, Wife of James, Born Dec. 25, 1836, aged 43 years, 9 months & 27 days.

MARGARET NELSON, Daughter of James & Elizabeth, May 22, 1868 - June 27, 1872.

Two infants NELSON, of James & Elizabeth, Died Oct. 10, 1871, aged 3 years.

LILABELLA NELSON, Daughter of James & Elizabeth, Born Aug. 1, 1863, Died Oct. 2, 1871.

Mrs. JANE NELSON, Mother of Nancy Caldwell, Died Nov. 19, 1870, aged 95 years

ROW 19

WILLIAM P. RADER, Born Nov. 23, 1835, Died April 24, 1847.

RALPH McFADDEN, Died Dec. 16, 1859, aged 50 years & 8 months.

SUSAN BUFORD McFADDEN, Died Feb. 7, 1868, aged 82 years.

JOHN K. GILL, Died Oct. 19, 1833, in the 45th year of his age.

JOHN GILL, Died Sept. 16, 1826, aged 43 years.

SAMUEL GILL, Died Feb. 5, 1840, in the 56th year of his age.

WILLIAM PORTER, Born Dec. 3, 1785, Died June 25, 1853, aged 67 years, 6 months & 22 days.

ESTHER JANE MILLER, Daughter of James W. & Sarah, Died May 21, 1854, aged 6 years & 7 months.

SAMUEL A. NEELY, Born Nov. 18, 1834, Died May 7, 1836.

MARGARET C. GILL, Born Sept. 12, 1841, Died Nov. 17, 1843.

JAMES DUNCAN, Died April 26, 1862, aged 63 years.

DORCAS J. NEELY, Daughter of John & Mary S., Born Dec. 28, 1829, Died Oct. 1833.

SARAH EDWARDS, Died Oct. 21, 1834, in her 65th year.

CHRISTOPHER S. GILL, Died Oct. 11, 1845, aged 48 years, 3 months & 15 days.

ELIZABETH A. GILL, Born Nov. 5, 1847, Died Oct. 8, 1848, aged 11 months & 3 days.

JOHN DUNLAP, Born June 20, 1794, Died Jan. 14, 1862, aged 67 years, 6 months & 24 days.

ELIZA S. GILL, Wife of J. G. B., Born Aug. 7, 1822, Died May 16, 1883.

J. G. B. GILL, Born Oct. 7, 1810, Died Aug. 18, 1878.

F. G. GILL, Born Jan. 16, 1859, Died Oct. 4, 1870.

SUSAN A. GILL, Died May 14, 1843, aged 8 months & 10 days.

MARTHA NEELY, Wife of Robert, Born Aug. 25, 1787, Died Sept. 13, 1861.

BENJAMIN F. CULP, CSA, Died Oct. 5, 1861, aged 21 years, 8 months, & 23 days.

ELIAS MILDOON, Died Aug. 23, 1822, aged 27 years.

RICHISON MILDOON, Died Sept. 6, 1841, aged 29 years.

ELIZABETH ROBINSON, Died July 20, 1845, aged 22 years.

MARY ROBINSON, Died Dec. 20, 1843, aged 61 years.

ROBERT ROBINSON, Died Nov. 8, 1842, aged 68 years.

JOHN S. NEELY, Died Mar. 16, 1838, aged 37 years, 5 months & 18 days.

MARY S. NEELY, Born Mar. 17, 1802, Died Oct. 27, 1855.

GEORGE GILL ROBINSON Nov. 1812 - April 1881

JAMES ROBINSON, Born April 1811, Died Aug. 1868.

NANCY GILL ROBINSON, Born Mar. 20, 1821, Died May 30, 1902.

MARTHA ANN REID, Died April 3, 1838, aged 10 months & 24 days.

SAMUEL LEONARD WHARRY, Died Aug. 14, 1815, aged 15 years.

GEORGE REID, Born May 8, 1803, Died May 20, 1855.

SARAH RODDEY, Born Mar. 1797, Died Sept. 15, 1873.

ELLEN DUNCAN, Born Oct. 31, 1795, Died June 21, 1884.

DAVID H. DUNCAN, July 20, 1820 - Nov. 12, 1882.

SARAH E. DUNCAN, Born July 24, 1818, Died Oct. 12, 1881.

MARIA LOUISA GILL, Daughter of L. H. & Jane Gill, Born Oct. 8, 1855, Died June 30, 1857.

ROW 20

MICHAEL STEEDMAN, Died Aug. 2, 1835 in his 79th year.

ROBERT NEELY, Died April 22, 1847, aged 65 years, 2 months & 8 days.

PATSY J. ROBINSON, 3d Daughter of R. & M., Born Dec. 12, 1816, Jan. 7, 1834.

ROBERT E. ROBINSON, Born Jan. 24, 1825, Died Dec. 31, 1851.

ROW 21

CHLOE E. STEELE, Born Feb. 1, 1851, Died Aug. 15, 1871.

SUSAN E. GILL, Wife of G. C., Born Sept. 15, 1827, Died Aug. 1875.

WILLIAM B. GILL, Born Sept. 13, 1860, Died Sept. 17, 1862.

THOMAS W. GILL, Son of G. C. & S. E., May 7, 1858.

ELIZABETH M. GILL, Born 1806, Died Aug. 21, 1856.

CHRISTOPHER S. GILL, Born Aug. 20, 1839, Died June 29, 1854.

MARGARET J. GILL, Born July 5, 1835, Died Oct. 28, 1853.

LOUISA A. GILL, Born Sept. 13, 1832, Died June 6, 1861.

SAMUEL CLARENCE NEELY, Son of W. R. & Maggie, Born Oct. 16, 1882, Died Oct. 12, 1894.

MAGGIE AGNEW NEELY, Wife of W. R., Born Oct. 3, 1857, Died June 25, 1887.

JOHNIE MAY NEELY, Daughter of J. G. R. & Mary, Born May 13, 1882, Died Sept. 11, 1882.

J. F. H. NEELY, Son of Samuel & Mary M., Born August 12, 1864, Died Sept. 10, 1875.

SAMUEL NEELY, Born Aug. 17, 1815, Died Jan. 4, 1866.

MARY M. WHITE, Wife of Samuel Neely, Born April 24, 1830, Died Sept. 19, 1904.

SAMUEL MARION NEELY, 1859 - 1906

MATTIE E. NEELY, Born June 8, 1866, Died Sept. 18, 1872.

MARTHA C. NEELY, Wife of W. W., Born Feb. 29, 1840, Died Aug. 12, 1866.

WILLIS W. NEELY, Born Mar. 24, 1832, Died June 20, 1869.

MARGARET A. McCULLOUGH, Daughter of John & S. E. Kelsey, Born Sept. 18, 1818, Died Sept. 1, 1861, aged 43 years & 17 days.

HARRIET ANN ROBINSON, Daughter of W. S. & E. F., Died Dec. 21, 1876, aged 23 years, 11 months & 21 days.

WILLIAM S. ROBINSON, Born Jan. 14, 1810, Died Oct. 27, 1882.

Mrs. E. F. ROBINSON, Born July 6, 1814, Died Feb. 12, 1886.

JAMES G. BRADFORD, son of James Mc. & M. J. Bradford, Born Feb. 13, 1872, Died Aug. 2, 1873.

MARGARET J. BRADFORD, Wife of J. M., Born Aug. 27, 1851, Died Dec. 18, 1875.

GEORGE BRADFORD, son of J. M. & E. S., Died July 5, 1880, aged 8 months.

ROW 22

ARCHIBALD STEELE, Born Feb. 17, 1788, Died May 24, 1865, aged 77 years, 3 months & 7 days.

MARTHA STEELE, Wife of ARCHIBALD, Born Feb. 1, 1797, Died ------ (headstone broken).

CHARLES B. STEELE, Born June 27, 1837, Died June 15, 1861, aged 20 years, 11 months & 12 days.

CHARLES L. BOYD, son of P. & Margaret, Born June 14, 1831, Died July 30, 1856.

WILLIAM J. STEELE, Son of W. A. & C. E., Born Feb. 1, 1871, Died May 30, 1871.

MARY R. STEELE, Daughter of W. A. & C. E., Born Aug. 24, 1869, Died April 7, 1870.

THOMAS P. GILL, Born June 20, 1796, Died Oct. 28, 1845, aged 50 years.

JOHNNY FARLEY, Son of W. F. & Julia A., Born Jan. 30, 1857, Died May 28, 1862.

TOMPSON HICKLIN KEE, Born Aug. 23, 1859, Died Sept. 8, 1860.

MARGARET E. KEE, Daughter of C. T. & Martha M., Born Oct. 22, 1841, Died Oct. 1, 1854, aged 12 years, 11 months & 9 days.

FRANCES G. MORGAN, Wife of Turner G., Died Mar. 3, 1853, aged 20 years, 5 months & 3 days.

SARAH C. McKNIGHT, Wife of Robert A. McKnight, Born April 19, 1827, Died July 16, 1854.

SUSAN J. MORGAN, Consort of T. G., Born May 5, 1837, Died July 18, 1857, aged 20 years, 2 months & 13 days.

WILLIAM DANIEL KIRKPATRICK, Son of Catherine & H., Born and Died May 2, 1859.

MARGARET FRANCES KIRKPATRICK, Daughter of Catherine H. & H., Born and died Mar. 13, 1861.

Mrs. C. H. KIRKPATRICK, Daughter of Wm. & Margaret Agurs, Died Nov. 9, 1876, aged 43 years, 10 months & 18 days.

MARGARET AGURS Born Dec. 6, 1798, Died May 9, 1878.

WILLIAM AGURS Born Aug. 7, 1784 Died March 7, 1864.

MARTHA M. DICKEY, Daughter of Harvey H. & Elizabeth Drennan, Born Aug. 8, 1844, Died May 22, 1871.

JOHN HARVEY DRENNAN, Son of H. H. & E. M., Born Mar. 9, 1848, aged 23 years.

JOHN H. GASTON, Born Dec. 20, 1813, Died Feb. 26, 1876.

D. G. GASTON, Born Nov. 30, 1856, Died Jan. 8, 1874.

JOSEPH A. GASTON, Born Mar. 4, 1810, Died Feb. 11, 1868.

MARTHA JANE GASTON, Born May 19, 1829, Died Dec. 10, 1857.

TOBITHA AGNES GASTON, Died Nov. 5, 1854.

ELIZABETH W. GASTON, Born Oct. 2, 1816, Died Oct. 11, 1850.

Infant GASTON, Daughter of J. A. & M. J., Died June 17, 1854.

JAMES GILL, Born Jan. 9, 1787, Died Oct. 29, 1852.

SARAH O. JOHNSTON, Born Sept. 7, 1813, Died Feb. 11, 1855.

JOHN JOHNSTON, Died Dec. 1869, in the 40th year of his age.

JOHN Q. A. GILL, Born Oct. 9, 1830, Died Mar. 9, 1855.

GEORGE W. GILL, Born July 22, 1822, Died Mar. 12, 1855.

THOMAS J. GILL, Born Jan. 1, 1828, Died Mar. 23, 1855.

ROW 23

MARY JANE BOYD, daughter of J. L. Martha M., Born Sept. 27, 1856, Died Nov. 4, 1856.

FRANCIS M. BOYD, Born Feb. 29, 1816, Died Jan. 25, 1858.

MATTIE CULP, Born June 4, 1885, Died Mar. 18, 1888.

FRANKIE CULP, Born April 24, 1882, Died July 5, 1887.

ROBERT N. CULP, Born April 4, 1835, Died April 14, 1907.

SUE T. CULP, Born Aug. 1, 1854, Died Sept. 19, 1947.

JANE KNOX, Daughter of J. W. R., Born April 29, 1882, Died Aug. 25, 1885.

FANNIE BELLE JORDAN, Daughter of G. W. & M. J. Jordan, Nov. 8, 1872 - Sept. 21, 1873

G. W. JORDAN, M.D., Born Oct. 17, 1835, Died Jan. 20, 1906.

MARGARET E. JORDAN June 25, 1870 - Oct. 12, 1932.

SARAH A. KELSEY, Born Nov. 17, 1822, Died Aug. 5, 1862.

MARY E. JOHNSTON, Born May 1, 1835, Died May 27, 1869.

MARGARET REBECCA BURDELL, Daughter of J. H. & M., Born Feb. 7, 1872, Died Sept. 18, 1880.

JOSEPH SAYE BURDELL, son of J. H. & M., Born Aug. 24, 1874, Died Sept. 27, 1882.

FLORENCE LILLIAN BURDELL, Died Feb. 8, 1879, aged 5 months, & 15 days.

JOHN BURDELL, Died Sept. 28, 1871, aged 2 years, 2 months, & 24 days.

SARAH MAHALA EAGLE, Daughter of J. E. & S. J., Born Sept. 27, 1867, Died Oct. 18, 1871.

WILLIE EAGLE, Son of J. E. & S. J., Born Mar. 20, 1870, Died Nov. 28, 1871.

JOHN ERASMUS EAGLE, Born Jan. 3, 1837, Died Dec. 24, 1871. Co. B, 53 N. C. Inf., CSA.

LAURA JANE EAGLE, Daughter of J. E. & S. J., Born Oct. 31, 1865, Died June 2, 1874.

SAMUEL McGATHEY, Born 1808, County Derry, Ireland, Died April 11, 1887.

NANCY McGATHEY, Born Mar. 1810, County Derry, Ireland, Died April 13, 1889, aged 79 years & 1 month.

ROW 24

WILLIAM RYAN, Died April 26, 1892, aged about 50 years.

MATTIE J. RYAN, Died Aug. 4, 1889, aged 24 years.

LOUISA FUDGE, Wife of Henry W. and Daughter of Nathaniel McCammon, Born Aug. 22, 1847, Died Nov. 20, 1871.

GEO. T. FUDGE, Son of H. W. & Louisa, aged 1 year & 9 months.

IRON FENCE

SUSAN DRENNAN, Wife of W. R., Born Feb. 28, 1854, Died Mar. 14, 1924.

Infant DRENNAN, Daughter of John H. & S. J., Died Jan. 6, 1896.

Infant DRENNAN, Son of R. F. & L. I., Born and died Aug. 24, 1894.

HARVEY H. DRENNAN, Died Aug. 10, 1890, aged 77 years.

ELIZABETH M. DRENNAN, Wife of Harvey H., Died Aug. 24, 1890, aged 73 years.

W. R. NEELY Sept. 23, 1856 - Feb. 5, 1921. Mason.

WITHIN COPING

CLAUDE E. STRAIT, Born July 13, 1884, Died July 6, 1941.

LUCY A. STRAIT April 8, 1892 - June 8, 1970

ISAAC LOUIS STRAIT, Born Oct. 30, 1888, Died Oct. 29, 1945.

Infant STRAIT, Son of Claude E. & Mary E., Born July 28, 1914, Died July 29, 1914.

MARY H. STRAIT Oct. 19, 1890 - March 15, 1967

MARY TURNER STRAIT, Wife of S. J., Born Sept. 3, 1852, Died Nov. 13, 1939.

NEWTON STRAIT, Born Mar. 13, 1837, Died Feb. 3, 1907.

SUSAN R. STRAIT, Wife of James Nelson, Born Aug. 24, 1839, Died May 6, 1910.

THOMAS LYLE STRAIT, Son of J. L. & L. J., Born Aug. 30, 1912, Died Sept. 6, 1913.

THOMAS J. STRAIT, Born Mar. 30, 1846, Died Nov. 17, 1916.

KNOWN BUT UNMARKED GRAVES

STEPHEN McELHENEY, Born 1758, Died Sept. 15, 1840.

Col. GEORGE GILL, Born 1761, New Jersey, Died July 8, 1844.

INDEX

Indexprepared by the authors and Miss Karon Mac Smith and Mrs. June Seay.

B

D

E

H

I

J

M

O

P

R

Y

Other Heritage Books by Brent H. Holcomb:

Bute County, North Carolina Land Grant Plats and Land Entries

CD: Early Records of Fishing Creek Presbyterian Church, Chester County, South Carolina, 1799-1859

CD: Kershaw County, South Carolina Minutes of the County Court, 1791-1799

CD: Marriage and Death Notices from The Charleston [SC] Observer, *1827-1845*

CD: South Carolina, Volume 1

CD: Winton (Barnwell) County, South Carolina Minutes of County Court and Will Book 1, 1785-1791

Early Records of Fishing Creek Presbyterian Church, Chester County, South Carolina, 1799-1859, with Appendices of the Visitation List of Rev. John Simpson, 1774-1776 and the Cemetery Roster, 1762-1979
Brent H. Holcomb and Elmer O. Parker

Kershaw County, South Carolina Minutes of the County Court, 1791-1799

Marriage and Death Notices from The Charleston Observer, *1827-1845*

Winton (Barnwell) County, South Carolina Minutes of County Court and Will Book 1, 1785-1791